Fodor's

P9-CFM-622

HOW TO PACK

SECOND EDITION

Fodor's Travel Publications
New York • Toronto • London • Sydney • Auckland
www.fodors.com

Fodor's HOW TO PACK

Editor: Karen Cure
Editorial Contributors: Laurel Cardone, Caroline Haberfeld, Holly Hughes
Editorial Production: Kristin Milavec
Production/Manufacturing: Robert B. Shields
Creative Director: Fabrizio La Rocca
Text and Cover Design: Guido Caroti
Illustrations: Alida Beck

COPYRIGHT

IMPORTANT TIP

All details in this book are based on information supplied to us at press time. But changes occur all the time in the travel world, and Fodor's cannot accept responsibility for facts that become outdated or for inadvertent errors or omissions. So **always confirm specifics as you plan your packing.** Specifically, call your airline to confirm baggage limitations and your outfitter or tour operator to confirm any must-haves for your trip.

SPECIAL SALES

Fodor's Travel Publications are available at special discounts for bulk purchases for sales promotions or premiums. Special editions, including personalized covers, excerpts of existing guides, and corporate imprints, can be created in large quantities for special needs. For more information, contact your local bookseller or write to Special Markets, Fodor's Travel Publications, 1745 Broadway, New York, NY 10019. Inquiries from Canada should be directed to your local Canadian bookseller or sent to Random House of Canada, Ltd., Marketing Department, 2775 Matheson Boulevard East, Mississauga, Ontario L4W 4P7. Inquiries from the United Kingdom should be sent to Fodor's Travel Publications, 20 Vauxhall Bridge Road, London, England SW1V 2SA.

PRINTED IN THE UNITED STATES OF AMERICA

10 9 8 7 6 5 4 3 2 1

Contents

INTRODUCTION:
WHAT MAKES A PACKING PRO? *VI*

1 **HOW TO BUY LUGGAGE** *1*

Look at Your Needs 3
Suitcases for All Travel Styles 5
Pullmans 6
Duffels 10
Garment Bags 12
Travel Packs 14
Laptop Luggage 17
Carry-On Luggage 20
How to Judge Quality 23

2 **YOUR TRAVEL WARDROBE** *31*

Thinking It Through 33
Know-How for Trips of All Kinds 47
Active Trips and Adventures 50
Active Trips in Hot Weather 50
Active Vacations in Winter 54
In the Mountains 56
Business Trips and Seminars 57
Casual Vacations 60
City Vacations 62
Cruises 64
Family Vacations 66
Resort Vacations 75
Theme Park Vacations 76

3 **THE PLAN** *78*

First Steps—Far Ahead 80
Check with Your Airline 80
Research Your Needs 84
Get Busy—Go Shopping 86
The Next Steps 95
Make Your Travel Kits 97

A Toiletries Kit 97
The Laundry Kit 103
The Sewing Kit 105
The First-Aid Kit 106
The Personal Documents Kit 107
The Portable Office 109
For Passionate Shoppers 111
Countdown to Packing. **113**
The Night Before 115
Get Packing! **117**
How to Fill Almost Any Suitcase 117
For Duffels and Travel Packs 125
Know-How for Garment Baggers 126
Practically Crease-Free Folding 132
About Your Carry-Ons 136
Savvy Checking **143**

4   **HOW TO PACK FOR THE WAY BACK   149**

Use Your Packing List 150
Dirty Laundry 150
The Paper Chase 152
Souvenir Savvy 153
VAT Refunds and Customs 155

5   **BAGGAGE PROBLEMS?   158**

The Drill 159
Damaged? 160
Delayed? 160
Officially Lost? 161

        APPENDIX:
        LUGGAGE & PACKING RESOURCES   163

Guidebooks 164
Family Stuff 164
General Packing Tips 165
Government Resources 165
Laptop Needs 166
Luggage Information 166
Passport Information 167

Technology Items and Info 167
Travel Goods Manufacturers and National
Retailers 168
Travel Insurance 172
Travel Packs and Outdoor Gear 173
VAT Refunds 174
Weather 174

INDEX   *175*

CHECKLISTS

Four Steps to the Perfect Suitcase 2
What to Look for in a Laptop Case 19
Luggage Features to Inspect 24
A Crash Course in Wardrobe Planning 32
Basic Wardrobe Options for Men 40–41
What to Wear on the Plane 45
Basic Wardrobe Options for Women 48–49
Ideas for Your Day Pack 51
Ideas for Hot Weather 53
Ideas for Cold Weather 56
Ideas for Mountain Trips 57
Kid Stuff to Bring 68–69
What to Put in Your Toy Tote 72
Top 10 Steps to No-Stress Packing 79
Top 10 Carry-On Tips 84
Travel Aids You May Want to Pack 94
What's in Your Toiletries Kit 99
What's in Your Laundry Kit 104
What's in Your Sewing Kit 105
What's in Your First-Aid Kit 107
What's in Your Personal Documents Kit 109
What's in Your Portable Office 110–111
Shopper's Survival Kit 112
Your Pretrip To-Do List 113
Your Night-Before To-Do List 115
Carry-On Musts 138
Carry-On No-Nos 139
Top 10 Checked-Luggage Tips 146

WHAT MAKES A
PACKING PRO?

"A journey of a thousand miles must begin with a single step," said Lao-tzu, the 6th-century BC philosopher. It's a lovely sentiment. But for most travelers, the first step is packing. And packing is more like a giant leap across a yawning chasm. An hour before leaving for the airport, they pull out a suitcase bought 10 years ago, blow into it, turn it over, shake it, and pronounce it garment ready. Then they pull out a bureau drawer and upend the contents into the suitcase. On top goes an iron, to eliminate wrinkles upon arrival.

Sitting on the suitcase to force it shut, wrestling with the fasteners, many of these same people swear there's got to be a better way. And there is.

You go to your closet and choose, from an extensive luggage collection, a bag that's just the right size for the trip, one that's loaded with nifty compartments that will keep clothing organized on the road. You line it with crisp, clean tissue paper and fill it strategically—guided by a carefully edited packing list prepared during the preceding two or three weeks—with freshly washed and ironed or dry-cleaned garments, each one carefully encased in plastic, shoes bagged and tidily filled with rolled undergarments and incidentals, and a toiletry kit that contains everything you need. The suitcase closes easily, nothing is left behind, and everything arrives as bandbox fresh as it was in your closet.

If you aspire to this vision, this book is for you.

This book will help you start a luggage wardrobe if you haven't already. It will help you expand your luggage wardrobe if you need to.

It will also help you with the critical planning that makes packing a breeze.

Our advice takes into account the practical realities of travel and of human nature. Although some pretrip packing strategies can be downright compulsive, we tell you about a few that can be real lifesavers, even for the shortest, most last-minute journey. Frequent travelers (and there are more and more of us these days) have plenty of tricks that pay off every time you travel. Some of these techniques save time, others save money, and still others save suitcase space and weight. (It's a wonderful feeling, being able to stroll right off the plane with an ultralight carry-on and go straight to the taxi stand, miles ahead of your fellow passengers.) Other tips pay off at your destination, when you find that you've got everything you need (and nothing more)—your clothes look great, everything matches, and your shoes don't hurt.

And here's the beautiful part: you can start getting ready now, even if you have no specific trip in the offing.

Different trips require different strategies, of course. The length of your journey, the season you're traveling in, the itinerary, the purpose of your trip, your mode of travel, whom you're traveling with—all must be factored in. In this book, you'll learn how to analyze your needs beforehand, so that you'll have the right suitcase and the right packing list every time. After all, you don't need the same clothes for a week of hiking in the Rockies that you do for a long weekend at a resort in Bermuda or a fortnight's theater-going in London.

One goal is uppermost: to make your packing a simpler first step so that, bags packed, you can move on to the fun part. Here's to a lifetime of rewarding journeys!

                                                        THE EDITORS

1

HOW TO BUY LUGGAGE

Perhaps you have been staving off the inevitable, borrowing luggage as often as you can, or using those inadequate, dilapidated bags just one more time while vowing you'll replace them before your next trip. Never fear: somewhere out there is the perfect bag with your name on it.

Dozens of manufacturers each produce dozens of styles. And each style comes in several different sizes, often in at least two different fabrics. Rolling carry-ons, which debuted in 1988, spawned a suitcase revolution that has been felt in every corner of the luggage department. Perhaps the great flash of inspiration that inspired the first one can all be traced back to the bellhop's dolly. Or perhaps it occurred when someone noticed the speed and dexterity with which flight attendants were able to race through the airport, gracefully pulling their baggage behind them on strap-on dollies. In any case, the innovation arrived just in time. With our peripatetic lifestyles, we need luggage that can keep up with us. Wheels certainly do the trick, so it's not surprising that wheeled suitcases have taken over in luggage stores and luggage departments all across America. The pullman, the rectangular container that has long been synonymous with the word "suitcase," is now most commonly seen in the vertical position, with wheels and a handle. Duffels have wheels, too, as do many backpacks—now known as "travel packs." The whole scene is vastly different from the one you would have encountered 10 years ago, or even five. And you can buy luggage almost everywhere, from luggage specialists to department stores to discount outlets and brick-and-mortar stores such as Wal-Mart and even Internet retailers.

FOUR STEPS TO THE PERFECT SUITCASE

- ❏ Assess your needs.
- ❏ Look at other people's luggage.
- ❏ Shop around—develop a short list.
- ❏ Compare quality and price.

Look at Your Needs

Ah, needs. Do any of us really spend enough time considering our own? Wouldn't it be great if you could really see all the clothes that you owned, so you'd know what you "needed" before you went shopping and came home with yet another black turtleneck? Well, if ever there was a time to stop and think about your needs it's before you go out to buy new luggage. Do you want your luggage to look attractive, suit your budget, or be ultradurable, light, and portable? Do you need something gigantic or do you want the smallest possible option? After you've decided what's essential, remember that in luggage, perfection is an illusion—a bag that has *most* of the qualities that matter to you is probably as close as you'll come. As in life, know what you need, go for what you want, and be willing to compromise.

WHAT TO THINK ABOUT Before you begin to zero in on particular brands and styles, take the time to consider how you like to travel. (And remember to revisit your assessment every few years—career moves, growing families, and changes in income can totally transform your travel habits.)

Consider when, how, and how often you will use the luggage. Do you plan to travel by air? by car? on a train or bus? How frequently do you expect to be taking trips? Do you usually travel alone, with a friend or partner, or with a family?

How frequently and how far will you need to transport your bag? Will you be checking it or lugging it through an airport to the gate as a carry-on piece? Do you think you may carry this suitcase yourself, or are you a person who hails porters whenever possible? Do you usually have a car waiting for you, or do you prefer public transportation?

If you're buying luggage for a specific trip, what is the nature of that trip? Do you expect to be traveling through several European countries by train, for which mobility will be crucial? Is there a cruise in your future? (You'll unpack the first evening, then kiss your bags good-bye for the duration of the voyage.) Do you take standard hotel trips, where bellhops are always on hand? Do you plan to hike and climb mountains with your luggage? Or will you be on the smooth streets of a big city?

How do you like to carry your luggage? Do you roll it, sling it over your shoulder, or strap it onto your back?

How do you pack? Do you prefer to hang your garments, roll them, or fold them? Do you always take more gear than you need, or do you rigorously prune down your packing list to a few essentials?

A LUGGAGE WARDROBE Think in terms of building a luggage wardrobe. Keep in mind the color, style, and function of the piece or pieces you own already, and make sure new items coordinate and serve a specific purpose. Buy pieces from different manufacturers, or stay with one line. Although some folks like to buy a whole set of luggage at once, others prefer to purchase an essential piece or two, and then add a new item as needed. The advantage of waiting is that you have an introduction to a line of luggage through your initial purchase; if you aren't pleased with its construction or durability, you won't be stuck with three other bags from the same manufacturer.

DO TALK TO STRANGERS

Whenever you're traveling, inspect fellow passengers' luggage to see what works. Don't be afraid to ask questions—people actually seem to *like* sharing luggage stories. Is that petite retiree easily trundling along with a massive suitcase on wheels? If so, the wheels and frame must be well designed. Is that stylish duffel on the hotel's luggage cart splitting open at the seams? Depend on it that the stitching and/or fabric just won't hold up when you do some serious traveling.

Suitcases for All Travel Styles

Wouldn't it be funny if instead of marking the passage of time by major life events such birthdays, graduations, marriage, and children, we measured it with the kind of luggage we used? Think of that first flowered cotton overnight bag that you brought to your cousin's sleep-over birthday party. OK, it was only across the street, but you were going away for the whole night—who knew what you might need? It was packed to bursting, but you carried it by yourself and besides, your father carried the sleeping bag and pillow.

Then in high school, you hauled your gear in suitcases borrowed from your parents on road trips to upstate New York and Rhode Island and a ski trip to Vail. Eventually, after graduation, it was your brother's big red backpack you took to Europe—you had to cut a deal with him to get it. Shiny aluminum frame and all, it was at least 3½ feet tall. Live and learn. Was it the getting married that did it or the fabulous trip you planned for your first anniversary?

CHECK OUT THE WHEELS

Poor Robert could have used wheels on his business trip to Italy, when he packed his clothing in three small duffels and several shopping bags. In his own words, his Oxford-cloth shirts wound up looking like "pressed flowers." A large suitcase with wheels would have been a better solution—even though it might have been heavier than his collection of small bags, it would have been far more maneuverable, because he'd have needed only one hand to manage it. Once you've narrowed your selection to several bags, take each one for a walk. Do you feel pressure on your back when you pull it? Is the handle at the right height, so that you don't have to crouch like a caveman dragging his club? Is most of the weight of the case balanced on the wheels, or are you carrying much of it yourself? Does the handle feel good in your hand? Increase your speed: does the bag begin to wobble? Stop suddenly: what happens? Choose that bag that feels the most comfortable.

At last, you decide it's time for luggage of your own. But which luggage? After months of searching, you go for the serious garment bag with the matching cabin bag, both in black nylon with grooved rubber patches. You're transformed. Cool. An adult at last. You have luggage, there's no place you can't go.

Of course, no matter which stage of life you're in, having the right luggage—luggage that fits your needs and your traveling style—can make all the difference between an average trip and a great one. Thinking about your options in advance will make it a lot easier for you to get there, too.

▶ Pullmans

Long ago, wealthy travelers transported their belongings in hard-side steamer trunks and hatboxes. But something happened on the way to the 21st century. These trunks didn't fit into the compact sleeping cars of America's trains, and a new suitcase style was born. A rectangular box with a hinged lid and a handle centered on the long open side, it was known as the pullman, named after the premier manufacturer of sleeping cars. Soon it became the suitcase of choice, and it still is for many travelers. But in almost every airport today, armies of travelers are wheeling so-called vertical or upright pullmans, which open just like the standard pullman but have wheels on one short side, and, on the other, a built-in telescoping handle and a second carrying handle. Large upright pullmans hold as much as a standard suitcase, and smaller ones can be wheeled aboard as carry-ons. If you're traveling with a family, you may choose to bring everybody's stuff in one big suitcase—in which case you'll definitely want it to have wheels. Some pullmans with wheels are cases and luggage carts in one; you simply place your computer case, briefcase, or a smaller tote on the extended handle. Easily handled as they are, they show you to be in control of your luggage, and if you're on a business trip, that's a good impression to make. And in a nifty twist, Samsonite has added extra wheels to either side of the case so that the bag can turn 90 degrees to roll easily where other suitcases might not fit—such as the

airplane aisle and tightly packed duty-free shops. Another Samsonite has a detachable pad that turns the top of the bag into a seat—a boon in long lines not to mention crowded airports.

Inside most pullmans, depending on the specific model, you'll find features that will help keep your clothing organized. Perfect for business travelers, "suiters" have a special compartment that opens to reveal a hanger bar for a suit or other dress clothes. Depending upon the dimensions of the case, it can accommodate two or three suits or several dresses and jackets. The garments are held in place by either a fabric strap or a padded bar, and the extra panel folds over in half or in thirds—which means that your clothing is folded only once or twice, and each fold is padded to prevent creases. On the opposite side, the suitcase opens up to reveal a compartment in which to store shirts, underwear, accessories, and toiletries.

A quick change in your hotel room on arrival and you look pressed, polished, and professional.

Other pullmans have simply one large, unstructured space inside, and, as a result, can accommodate themselves to many packing styles. They work just as well for rolled-up dungarees and T-shirts as for jackets, trousers, blouses, and other easily wrinkled items. These pullmans come with wheels and without, and in sizes ranging from humongous to small enough to fit under an airplane seat.

DON'T OVERPAY

Once you've narrowed your choices to a particular make or model, go comparison shopping for the best price. Luggage sales occur throughout the year, so look for advertisements in your local newspaper. In addition to price discounts, manufacturers often include a matching toiletry kit or day pack as an incentive, or feature two pieces—such as a garment bag and a carry-on bag—at a special price that's less than what they would normally cost if purchased separately. Some stores sell look-alike but lower-end models at "reduced" prices; should you come across a surprisingly low price, do a hands-on inspection to make sure it's the exact model you want. Check the number of inside divisions, and look closely at important details such as handle and wheel construction. Also open each suitcase, examine all the various compartments, and decide how you would arrange your clothing inside. Remember: it may be the top-selling model in the country, but it's your opinion that matters—if it doesn't please you, you'll regret your purchase every time you travel.

SOFTIES For years, travelers have debated the comparative virtues of soft- and hard-side pullmans. Which you prefer is entirely a matter of personal preference. Today's soft-side suitcases are made of fabrics ranging from Cordura and other durable synthetics to leather, vinyl made to look like leather, elaborate tapestry nylons, and nylon tweeds; these are usually stretched over a full or partial frame.

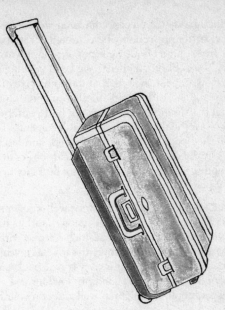

Innovative designs as well as strong, lightweight fabrics have made soft-side bags as durable as their hard-side cousins, and they weigh less. Soft-side luggage tends to be flexible enough to allow you to squeeze in that last precious souvenir; once hard-side luggage is packed, it's packed. And although soft-side pieces may appear to be flimsier than hard-side ones, if they're thrown around (and they will be) they actually absorb shocks better than hard-side bags. Soft-side luggage made of good-quality ballistic nylon—this is similar to the stuff used in bulletproof vests—is virtually impossible to puncture or slash (*see* How to Judge Quality, *below*).

A HARD ACT TO FOLLOW Suitcases made of shiny aluminum and of molded materials such as polypropylene and ABS plastic have edged out earlier hard-siders, which were traditionally made of cardboard or plywood covered with fabric, leather, or vinyl and bound with leather or vinyl at the

seams. Such hard-side pieces, compared with soft-side suitcases, offer better protection when crushed or sat upon; if you
plan to carry around bisque figurines or other breakables, it's
the best choice. Photographers have been packing their expensive camera gear in stylish aluminum boxes for years.
These cases, along with others in other materials, now come
with wheels. Aluminum suitcases are both waterproof and
fireproof—just the thing for important documents. They cannot be slashed open like some fabric bags, and last virtually
forever. On the downside, the metal can be scratched and
dented, and it makes for a case that is a bit hefty even when
empty.

THE ULTIMATE SUITCASE One well-known manufacturer of adventure luggage offers its own, rather nifty convertible version of the standard 22-inch suitcase with wheels:
a zip-out panel folds down to cover the wheels, revealing back
straps that convert the bag into a travel pack. After all,
wheels won't do you much good on a wilderness trail, and
what you can't pull you might as well carry on your back.

▶ Duffels

Santa Claus uses a duffel. So do postal workers. So do all
those young men in uniform you see in scenes from 1940s
movies; as they share a farewell embrace with loved ones, a
heavy canvas bag, stuffed to bursting, stands waiting on the
porch.

Duffels have terrific portability. Soft-sided and frameless,
they're just right when you're packing casual clothing. They're
lighter and cost less than most traditional suitcases. They're
easy to carry by hand or over the shoulder. And they're end-
lessly forgiving when you have a bit too much to pack. As a result, they make excellent vacation bags—many people feel
they can pack for a two-week trip in a duffel that slips under
an airplane seat. Duffels are especially good when you're traveling with children—their things generally don't need as
much protection as adult clothes.

Some duffels, particularly larger ones, also come with wheels and a telescoping handle. This type of bag still looks sporty, but has a slightly more professional air than a typical duffel.

THE BAG THAT GROWS Duffels are sized by cubic inches of space: A typical carry-on model has a capacity of about 2,500 cubic inches, and a full-size one between 3,500 and 4,500 cubic inches (larger ones are available). But some duffels also have an expansion segment—an extra 5 or 6 inches of space at the end or bottom of the bag that can be freed by zipper so that the bag can "grow" when needed. This is especially handy when you're returning home with more than you originally packed. It also makes for a more flexible piece of luggage; because you can choose which size to use, you don't need two separate bags.

WHAT'S INSIDE Bare-bones duffels generally have a single compartment and no outside pockets. Upscale versions, made of more substantial fabric—ballistic nylon, Cordura, or Cordura Plus—generally have separate compartments at either end for shoes and accessories, and perhaps an outside pocket or two.

Some duffels are equipped with hidden back and waist straps that convert them into travel packs. Easy to carry as a duffel may be when you're walking down the street, it's great to

have the option of backpacking when the terrain gets rougher
or when you need your hands free (to hold your child's hand,
perhaps). Because they don't have frames, these won't be as
comfortable as a full-scale travel pack when you're carrying
heavy loads, but they can be marvelous in a pinch.

OVER THE RAINBOW In terms of color, duffels have certainly come out of the closet in recent years, even more so than
other types of luggage. Day-Glo colors abound, but conservative travelers, take heart—duffels still come in basic black,
brown, navy, and green. While remembering the colors of your
other luggage, you can be a little adventurous. A bright-red,
safety-orange, or lemon-yellow duffel trimmed in black might
look smashing alongside your businesslike black pullman.

▶ Garment Bags

Garment bags are luggage for grown-ups: your clothes have
to be tall before you need a suitcase that folds over in half.
Pullmans can carry full-length suits, too, but garment bags do
a better job, and most have many useful features that you
don't find in those flimsy bags you get when you buy a new
suit or a formal gown at a department store. Adored by business travelers, garment bags are also useful if you're going on a
cruise or heading for an out-of-town wedding or anywhere
else that requires clothing that needs special attention.

LOOK AT FEATURES AND LENGTH

When shopping, compare the interiors of several bags. Consider
whether the space allocation makes sense to you. Would you prefer to have fewer restrictions? Also spend some time experiment-
ing in the store to see which size works best. Garment bags come
in several different lengths, the longest up to 56 inches. This
may not be an issue for men who are packing only suits, but for
a woman, a short bag means that the hems of longer dresses
and coats must be folded back. A taller person should have no
trouble carrying a 45-inch bag; someone of average height may
feel more comfortable with one that measures 40 inches.

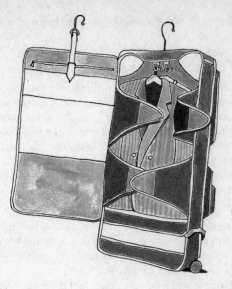

CARRY-ON ARMOIRES If you use a garment bag, you can pack straight from your closet, then unpack simply by unfolding the bag and hanging it in the closet in your hotel. Because of the bag's shape, your clothing can be folded fewer times, reducing the possibility of wrinkles.

Polished, professional, and often lighter than pullmans, garment bags are also ideal as carry-ons; you can either hang them in the cabin closet or fold them over and place them in the overhead compartment. (Slim garment bags made of light nylon are particularly handy, especially for overnight business trips.)

If you're using it as your main piece of luggage, you'll probably want a sturdy model made of a heavier fabric and roomy enough to hold enough clothes for a two-week trip. This kind of garment bag is generally longer, has inside and outside pockets for stowing other garments and accessories, and comes with locks. For ultimate flexibility, you may want to purchase both a lightweight garment bag and a heavy-duty one.

OPEN SESAME? Most bags open like books, but others have a flap that unzips and folds down to let you get at your clothing. Some variations on this theme are more successful than others. In a third design, where the flap opens on the diagonal, reaching everything can be tricky. Yet another style requires that you unzip horizontal zippers top and bottom as well as a perpendicular one down the center. This can be inconvenient and time-consuming. Some models have a handy fold-out accessories panel that can be detached and hung in the closet by itself.

VARIATIONS ON A THEME Whereas some garment bags are bags pure and simple, others are divided into compartments to help you organize your things. Some have interior pockets of various sizes, often made of mesh so you can find items quickly and easily. Although garment bags typically fold in half, some newer models fold in thirds, producing a smaller and more portable package (although this also means more folds in your clothing). Some bags have wheels. High Sierra, a well-known manufacturer of adventure luggage, makes a tri-fold garment bag that has zip-out backpack straps and a zip-on day pack on the outside.

▌ Travel Packs

When the hordes of America's baby-boom generation first descended upon Europe in the late '60s and '70s, student visas and Eurail passes in hand, they were called backpackers. They all carried lumpy Army-surplus packs with just enough room for a second pair of jeans, a couple of extra flowered shirts, and maybe (or maybe not) some underwear. These packs were ideal hippie gear, easy to sling into the backseat of someone else's car or to use for a pillow if you were sleeping in a train station overnight. But the Aussies and Germans who were going the same route had something still

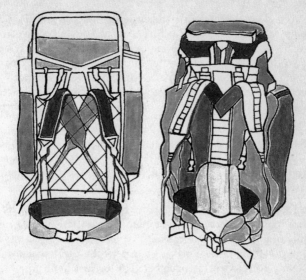

better; their packs were made of waterproof nylon and had hollow aluminum frames. Americans were quick to switch to these lighter packs and have been using them ever since. But like most other toys of the baby-boom generation they've been upscaled, upsized and downsized, and high-teched in every way imaginable by smart manufacturers who know a good market when they see one.

The new travel packs, a.k.a. backpacks, simply can't be beat for rugged vacations—rugged being trips that have you hauling your belongings for miles at a time, through swampland or down the endless streets of the urban jungle. Packs are great for casual vacation clothing, and they project an air of romantic independence—getting one is kind of like opting for a Harley-Davidson over a minivan. But like minivans, they're forgiving when you want to stuff in just one more thing. They leave your hands free so that you can hold a map, take notes, or help a child. And although they're generally lighter than some other kinds of suitcases, many have a strategically placed handle that lets you pack and carry them like a pullman. Packs are also a good family solution—get them for your youngsters so that they may carry their own gear. Some packs can morph into a suitcase with wheels.

SIZE Like duffel bags, packs are measured in cubic inches. There's a 3,200-cubic-inch carry-on size, and for more serious treks you can opt for a capacity of 5,100 or 6,000 cubic inches.

STRUCTURE Not all packs are equal. Some have an exterior frame of lightweight aluminum. These are really best for mountain climbers and campers. Others have a very flexible internal frame, which makes them perfect for trips when you simply want to feel unencumbered by luggage. Yet before you make a choice, you need to be clear about the type of travel you're planning.

TRY PACKS ON FOR SIZE

If you want a backpack, head for the nearest outdoors store—REI, Patagonia, and Eastern Mountain Sports are a few of the options. In the store, imagine yourself packing. Can you fit what you need into this space? Open several packs to see whether you like the way the space has been divided. Compare features to be sure you're getting what you want. And be persistent: Try on as many packs as you need to, so that you can get a sense of how they feel. Are you comfortable bearing the burden on your back? Be sure to adjust the straps to suit your body size and to alleviate any possible pressure or discomfort. Remember that if the pack isn't comfortable empty, it's going to make you miserable when it's full. If the pack has wheels, make sure that the handle is comfortable to pull.

WHAT'S COOL Some packs are designed specifically for women, taking into account their smaller size in the placement and adjustability of the straps. Convertibility is another definite plus in a travel pack; a zippered panel can hide back and waist straps to magically transform packs into more traditional-looking luggage. Most packs have a large central compartment and outside pockets, and some also have extra removable pouches. Many packs also come with a removable day pack; when attached it functions as a pocket, but unzip it and—voilà!—it's a separate bag that you can carry around for an afternoon of sightseeing or a morning on the trails. Some packs have an expandable main compartment that zips open to provide extra room for souvenirs or some cheese and a loaf of bread. One High Sierra pack, a nifty convertible version of the standard backpack with wheels, has a zip-out panel that folds down to cover the wheels, revealing back straps that convert the bag into a travel pack. After all, wheels won't do you much good on a wilderness trail, and what you can't pull you might as well carry on your back.

▶ Laptop Luggage

With the advent of notebook computers, doing your work while you fly is as simple as can be. Some airports and airport clubs are equipped with modem ports so you can go on-line between flights; some aircraft are equipped with 15V DC power outlets (these are either on the seat console or mounted to the seat frame below the cushion, usually in first and business class but sometimes in coach as well). You can run your laptop computer or your portable CD player or DVD player; all you need is a power adapter cord from your local electronics store.

You're better off looking for a case for your laptop in a computer store or a retailer that specializes in laptop cases; there are several on the Internet. Your choices are generally sup-

ple black leather or black canvas, both of which go with
anything. When buying a computer carry-on case, look for a
light frame and plenty of protective padding as well as a
shoulder strap and a briefcase-style handle that are securely
attached. Inside there should be straps and movable dividers
to keep your computer snugly positioned in transit, as well
as compartments for your portable printer, docking station,
transformers, and spare hard drives, and easy-to-access pockets to hold disks, books, papers, and pens. The closing
should be secure—perhaps a sturdy zipper. Most computer
carry-ons are essentially only modified attaché cases, but a
few manufacturers offer backpack-style models with a pair
of adjustable shoulder straps. These are great if you plan to
bicycle or hike and want to take your computer along,
though they don't have the boxy shape that conforms so
snugly to the computer.

WHAT TO LOOK FOR IN A LAPTOP CASE

- ❑ Plenty of padding
- ❑ Interior straps and dividers
- ❑ A comfortable shoulder strap
- ❑ A good handle
- ❑ Inside compartments and pockets
- ❑ A secure closing

AVOID AIRPORT SCAMS

When carrying your computer through airport security check-points, you'll have to lay it down on the X-ray belt to be scanned. Although some computer experts warn that repeated scans may damage the hard drive, passengers rarely have a choice nowadays. Tip #1: Don't put your laptop on the conveyer belt until the person in front of you has gone through the metal detectors. Tip #2: Don't let anyone distract you once your computer has started moving on that belt. Move promptly through the body check and be ready to pick up your computer as soon as it emerges from the scanner. Airport thieves, working in pairs, know this is a ripe opportunity for lifting laptops. Tip #3: Add a colorful bandanna or luggage tag to the handle, or strips of bright duct tape to the sides to eliminate the possibility of another business traveler mistaking your black laptop case for his or her own. Tip #4: Keep your laptop charged. You will probably be asked to turn it on, to prove that it is what it seems to be.

Many luggage manufacturers have addressed the fact that so many people now travel with their laptops by creating computer bags that fit in with their other lines of luggage. For

instance, the Zipoff series from Lodis allows various interchangeable bags to be added to a basic carry-on. Outside
the Overnighter, a carry-on, are a removable, zip-off computer case and a pouch that becomes a fanny pack. In
McKleinUSA's R series, the handles and wheels of the
rolling computer case can be detached—bingo, you have a
standard computer case. Brenthaven makes backpacks that
have extra padded computer sleeves. One model even adds
shock absorbers on the wheels.

▶ Carry-On Luggage

Look around you on your next trip. You'll be surprised at how
many people, even those with a mountain of matching luggage, stuff their on-board items into any old bag they can
find.

Proper carry-on bags should be a carefully considered part of
everyone's luggage wardrobe. This may include some kind of
roll-aboard suitcase. But it should also include some kind
of tote bag or backpack. Even if you do check most of your
belongings, you'll probably want to bring some things into
the cabin with you—valuables, a camera, reading material for
the flight, your toiletry kit, medicine, and toys and snacks if
you're traveling with children. Depending on the size of this
bag, you can also carry it around when you attend meetings or
see the sights. Maps, travel guides, cameras, passports, phrase
books—they do add up. Get a carry-on tote that can double
as a daily tote bag and you've got it made.

In a way, carry-ons are not a separate category of luggage at
all, but a subset of the others: there are carry-on garment
bags, carry-on duffels, carry-on travel packs, even carry-on
suitcases with wheels. To these can be added a fifth type, the
carry-on tote, which can be opened at the top to allow easy
access to your stuff. The defining element is size.

Carry-on luggage works well for both business and pleasure
trips. A 20- to 22-inch suitcase with wheels with a suiter

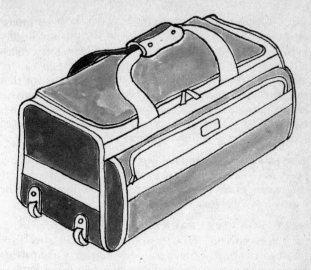

compartment is perfect for formal business trips, as are light-weight garment bags designed to carry suits, dresses, and formal wear with a minimum of wrinkling. Garment bags don't fit under the seat, but they can be stowed either in the overhead compartment or in the front of the cabin. For vacationers, mid- to small-size duffels and travel packs also function well as carry-ons, fitting either under the seat or overhead.

In the store, check out the same details you would on a full-size pullman, garment bag, duffel, or travel pack. Then practice carrying several different styles. Consider how you prefer to tote a bag. Are you most comfortable rolling it, slinging it over your shoulder, or holding it by a handle? If a bag offers more than one carrying option, all the better.

HOW BIG CAN YOU GO? The main plane requirement is that a bag be small enough to fit either in the overhead bin or under the seat in front of you. The dimensions should total 45 inches: 20 x 16 x 9, for example, or 21 x 13 x 8, or 22 x 14 x 9.

With so many travelers opting for carry-ons these days, snagging compartment space on a sold-out flight is not for the faint of heart. Although the space at your feet is not as large, remember that it's yours and no one else's. So it's wise to make your primary carry-on one that fits under the seat. For this purpose, smaller is definitely better; in many planes, a leg underneath the aisle seat and the fuselage's curvature alongside window seats mean that you will find unencumbered space for a carry-on only underneath center seats.

Also remember how endless airport terminal concourses can be. A carry-on has to be easy to carry on, or it doesn't deserve the name. That's all the more true if you plan to use the carry-on as a day pack for sightseeing.

HELP FOR OVERPACKERS Whether you're trying to cram in everything for your trip or just using your carry-on to take care of overflow from your other luggage, expandability is a plus. Soft-side bags generally function best in the carry-on realm, so if you've opted for hard-side in the rest of your luggage, shop around for something soft-sided that coordinates decently with the rest of your bags instead of a matching carry-on.

Note that although a light frame can be helpful in protecting your belongings—especially in a garment bag—it's a good idea to avoid anything too heavy to carry or too rigid to fit into the spaces provided on aircraft.

Consider how and what you'll be packing into your carry-on, and how many different compartments you'll want. If you intend to carry all your trip gear in your carry-on, you'll need a bag that can tidily store clothes as well as toiletries and reading material. It's also a good idea to have some outside pockets to hold items you may want to get at midflight.

THE GORILLA TEST You may think that a carry-on needn't be as durable as your other bags, since you'll always be the one handling it. But what happens when your fellow passengers start "rearranging" the overhead compartment? When the flight attendant "assists" you by shoving your overstuffed duffel farther under the seat in front of you? Or when you're asked to check your carry-on—the airline's prerogative? You'll still want a fabric that will hold up well, either a supple leather or a sturdy nylon or canvas (remember the importance of portability).

Zippers and clasps should be as sturdy as on other types of luggage. Although locks may not be as critical, remember that even if you never check this bag, you may have to leave it unattended in a hotel baggage room or elsewhere at your destination.

How to Judge Quality

The story went something like this: You bought a sporty new garment bag to take on a long weekend to Paris. At the baggage carousel after landing back in New York, you were horrified to see what approached: your poor little bag had a mangled shoulder strap. When you bent over to slip the strap over your shoulder, the part attached to the garment bag tore right off. You were crestfallen, but continued to use the bag for several more years. (Oh, all right, you're still using it.) During another trip, you met a man traveling with the same garment bag, also sans shoulder strap. Apparently, his, too, had given up the ghost early on. Does anyone see a structural flaw here?

The point is that not all bags are created equal. Luggage varies tremendously. Although people who travel only occasionally may not need the same level of durability as those who check their luggage many times each month, even seldom-used luggage takes a beating—and nobody wants to retrieve a shredded bag on the baggage carousel or have a suitcase fall apart midtrip. In any case, you should know what you're getting for the money you're spending. And don't pay top dollar for bottom-of-the-barrel quality.

So carefully compare luggage from different manufacturers and even different pieces within a single line. Open the bag in the store and look closely at how it's made.

HOW'S THE FRAME? Fiberglass inner structures (frames) ensure both light weight and strength. Inner structures may also be made of aluminum, wood, durable molded plastic compounds, or any combination of the above. A weighty frame will make a case heavy even before it's packed. Frame materials are often listed on the luggage tag; your friendly neighborhood luggage salesperson should also be able to tell you what they are.

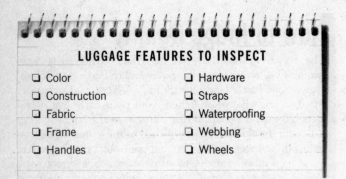

LUGGAGE FEATURES TO INSPECT

❏ Color   ❏ Hardware
❏ Construction   ❏ Straps
❏ Fabric   ❏ Waterproofing
❏ Frame   ❏ Webbing
❏ Handles   ❏ Wheels

IS THE CONSTRUCTION GOOD? On cases with zippers, look for taped seams, in which a strip of cloth reinforces the zipper and bag connection; this prevents fraying. On the outside of the bag, joints should be covered with either leather or nylon piping or welts to reinforce the seams and absorb wear and tear. Also, seams should be lockstitched, a method in which each stitch is reinforced, or locked, to stay in place and stand alone. (Look for the loop around each individual stitch.) This way, if one stitch happens to break, it won't take the next one with it and unravel your seam.

WILL THE FABRIC HOLD UP? Fabric counts for a lot in luggage. Leather luggage—long a status symbol, no matter whose initials it's embossed with—can be very durable and looks marvelous (until it gets scuffed, that is), but it is often too heavy to be carried even when it's empty. Top-grain or full-grain leather, the outermost layer of the hide, is stronger and more durable than leather made from splits, the layers of hide that are split off from underneath the top grain. Luggage made from splits costs less but is more likely to show wear.

Among the various fabrics available, those that are heavier protect the bag's contents better and stand up to sharp objects that might cause tears or rips in transit. Popular these days are ballistic nylon and Cordura nylon. Ballistic nylon is a bit more expensive but worth it. The same bag made of Cordura or Cordura Plus costs less and is still pretty sturdy. Although tweed and brocade bags may appear sturdier than nylon ones, they are slashable and the thicker fabric adds weight.

Among luggage connoisseurs, the denier, or thickness, of the yarn used in the fabric is a major issue. The higher the denier, the stronger the yarn and the fabric woven from it. Unfortunately, it's difficult to compare denier from bag to bag. Some manufacturers do not list it on their informational tags, and even luggage salespeople are often unable to determine what it might be. The important thing to keep in mind is that few bags on the market are made of fabric woven from less than 400-denier yarn; many fabric yarns are between 400- and 1,000-denier, and a few are as high as 2,000-denier. If your bag pleases you in all other ways, don't sweat the denier.

There are some other unusual fabrics that are perfect for the traveler concerned about the environment. These include Fortrel EcoSpun, a durable material made from recycled plastic bottles, and fabric woven from hemp.

Choose fabric in a color that you like and that harmonizes with any other luggage you own. Keep in mind that lighter colors show stains faster, whereas darker colors are more likely to show dust.

MONSOON-PROOF? Whether you're trapped in an Indian monsoon or a steady Seattle downpour, or you've got your luggage on a cartop carrier the day the hurricane blows through, waterproof luggage comes in handy. Poor Jackie had an incident in which her black canvas bag was drenched. When she unpacked, she discovered that all her light-colored clothing had been dyed to match the bag. How to avoid this? The best all-around fabric would be a Cordura or ballistic nylon with a waterproof seal—most bags are not waterproofed on the outside, but treated on the inside with a moisture-resisting sealant. Check the informational tag on the luggage or ask the salesperson to explain how the bag has been waterproofed. If you require special protection from water for camping, rafting, or some other adventure expedition, buy at a store that specializes in more rugged gear; the salespeople at places like this can often discuss the relative merits of manufacturers and their luggage from their own personal experience on trips like the one you're planning.

LOOK AT THE CLOSINGS The simpler, the better. If there's a zipper, it should be tough and run smoothly. Zippers should also be double-stitched (stitched on both sides of the zipper) and self-repairing or large, very sturdy, and smooth-running. Zippers made of polyester coils that have been woven or sewn to tapes can take a lot of pressure and can be healed if they pop open. Large zipper pulls are always easier to work with.

GET LOCKS You should also be able to lock your bag. Small combination locks, which are designed for luggage, may come on hard-side pullmans and are a plus if you tend to lose keys. The more rivets or screws that attach it to the case, the more secure the lock will be.

TEENY TINY ZIPPER PULLS?

If the pulls on your suitcase are small, attach large paper clips to them so you can get a better grip.

Luggage that closes with two-way zippers may come with small locks designed to hook through the zipper pulls on each compartment.

GET A GRIP ON THE HANDLES Handle construction may well be the most overlooked detail, and yet it is crucial—whatever the style of luggage. Be sure to pick up the suitcase, and make sure that it's comfortable in your hand; any slight discomfort will be magnified when it's fully loaded.

On a pullman, and on garment bags (at the fold), look to see whether the handle is attached to the bag with screws or with rivets. (A handle attached with screws can be replaced; when a riveted handle comes off, it's down for the count.) Also note whether the handle is padded on the underside, and whether it's covered with leather or only sturdy plastic.

For upright pullmans and duffels, count how many handles there are on the bag: is there one on the side as well as on the top? Side handles are a great help when you're lifting the bag onto a closet shelf or into an overhead compartment on a plane. On travel packs, in addition to the back straps, there should be handles on at least two sides of the bag.

Most suitcases with wheels are equipped with a telescoping handle that pulls out of the case when needed. Some handles can be locked in place, whereas others remain free to slide in and out at random. The handle system should be well protected, whether it's housed inside the bag or outside. (Not all handles measure up, however. Be sure the handle is sturdy, especially if you plan to hang a briefcase or tote bag over it). Pull the handle out and tilt the bag; watch to see whether it stays rigid. If it bends at all it is probably too weak to take any more weight. In addition, handles that run inside the bag can take up some of your precious packing space. How much this matters depends on how big your bag is and how much space you're giving up.

CHECK THE STRAPS AND WEBBING Shoulder straps for duffels and garment bags should be made of wide webbing, and ideally they should be padded where they rest on your shoulders. Note how the webbing is attached to the bag. Is it reinforced with box and cross stitching? Choose a duffel with a shoulder strap in addition to two center handles—this increases your carrying options for times when you'll need your hands free. When shopping around, ignore salespeople who give you nasty looks, and spend some time adjusting the straps and handles to suit your size. If the duffel doesn't hang well from your shoulder, or seems unwieldy when held by its handle, you'll want to know now, not the day of the trip.

On pullmans, notice where the handles are placed. It is helpful to have both side and top handles, for easier portability.

It's equally important for the straps of travel packs to be padded, because they will be resting on your shoulders for long periods of time. Look for a padded waist or hip strap as

well, to steady and center the bag on your body. All straps should be adjustable for height and weight.

TEST THE WHEELS If the wheels don't work on a piece of wheeled luggage, you might as well have bought a regular pullman. Four wheels make a suitcase more stable and easier to roll than do two wheels (think car versus motorcycle). The wheels should also be spaced as widely apart as possible and at least slightly recessed into the bag's frame so that it provides some protection for them—an exposed wheel can be neatly severed from your bag by a pothole, an uneven cobblestone, or a seemingly innocuous curb. Large, sturdy in-line-skate wheels provide the ultimate in rollability and performance. Insist on smooth-rolling wheels that are firmly bolted in place.

INSPECT THE HARDWARE In garment bags, pay special attention to the brackets that hold the clothes hangers in place. Some bags come with two brackets, which allows you to form alternative layers of clothing and cuts down on wrinkles. The hook that you'll hang the bag from should be well secured when not in use: Does it retract into the bag, snap tight to the bag, or dangle uselessly and dangerously? Is the hook itself strong or flimsy? Remember that it must bear the weight of the entire bag when hung in a closet. Also consider the clothes hangers. Are there enough of them? Or can you use your own? It's handiest if you can move your garments straight from your closet into the bag, without having to switch hangers.

WHAT'S INSIDE? Are there straps to hold clothing in place? In garment bags, look for models that have two straps that crisscross over the top half of the clothing as well as a center strap. These really do keep your things from sliding around and wrinkling.

2

YOUR TRAVEL
WARDROBE

Savvy globetrotters seem to know instinctively how to travel with less. If you're seriously disciplined, you could conceivably go for months at a time with one of those small shoulder-strap cabin bags the airlines used to give away as perks. Just add T-shirts, one or two pairs of trousers and shorts, some underwear, and minimal supplies for laundry. George economizes on luggage because he uses crutches to get around, but packing light

A CRASH COURSE IN WARDROBE PLANNING

- ❑ Research weather and local customs.
- ❑ Stick to one color scheme.
- ❑ Make clothes do double duty.
- ❑ Plan on doing laundry.
- ❑ Try on each outfit.
- ❑ Accessorize.
- ❑ Eliminate.

enables him to travel on his own terms. And oh, the places he goes!

Of course, not all travelers want to live out of a cabin bag. There are times when you want, or need, to have a bit more with you. If you're in the fashion or design business, in which wearing the same pair of shoes three nights in a row is right up there with mixing stripes and polka dots, you'll want to take a more extensive wardrobe. Cruise vacations, at least on larger ships, are another time to pack more lavishly—your luggage remains on board for the entire voyage, and that extra evening dress or dinner jacket will help you experience the deluxe side of shipboard life to the hilt.

PART TECHNIQUE, PART TRAVEL PHILOSOPHY

There is something important to be learned by studying George's approach to travel—he simply won't let his gear get him down. Streamlining your packing means that you are in control of your luggage instead of at its mercy. (Think of a dog leading its master next time you go to an airport. You'll definitely see people being led by their bags.) Take a cue from business travelers, who have learned to travel with nothing but carry-on luggage. And having discovered the freedom of traveling with carry-on luggage only, they often prefer to pack that way for personal vacations as well. Having landed in a strange place without so much as a Handi-Cart to greet you, it's nice to know you can manage on your own. Less physical baggage can often mean less emotional baggage, as well; in today's complicated world there's an exhilarating feeling of freedom and lightness that comes from living out of just one bag.

This sensation is your goal as you begin to plan your wardrobe.

Remember, lists can be used at least twice—once to pack and once to repack—so you'll be sure to remember to take home everything you've brought with you. You'll also have a record of the contents of your suitcase. Just in case.

Thinking It Through

Start planning your wardrobe by considering what the trip is all about. Is this a business trip on which you'll dress to impress at daylong meetings and seminars? A cruise or a resort vacation where nice casual clothing is the order of the day? Or a stay at a dude ranch where anything dressier than jeans would be totally out of place? A family vacation during which you and your children may be kneeling in the grass to make rubbings of gravestones or going between beach and beach house all day every day? A honeymoon someplace where you and your love will wear nothing more than matching sarongs? Will you be seeing the same people for the duration, or meeting new ones every few days? Do you want to look stylish or are you roughing it? In each case, you'll want a slightly different wardrobe.

As your itinerary comes together, make a day-by-day schedule of your mornings, noons, afternoons, and evenings, and next to each activity note possible outfits, including shoes and accessories. For a business trip for a travel journalist, these notes might read as follows: Morning: breakfast, six hotel site inspections, lunch—yellow sundress, sun hat, brown sandals, silver earrings. Afternoon: rafting down the Martha Brae River—pink bathing suit, orange T-shirt, khaki shorts, sneakers, sunglasses.

MAKE A LIST

The wish list, the wait list, the black list, the "A" list . . . some-times it seems our lives are governed by lists. But they really do come in handy when packing, especially when you're prepar-ing for a last-minute trip. After the 42.5% of the respondents to a recent Fodor's survey who are last-minute packers, the next-largest group—29%, nearly one-third of those surveyed—declare that they make lists and pack at least one week before a trip. Somehow even a mental list is never quite as effective as an actual list written on a piece of paper. Check the basic wardrobe lists in this chapter to ensure you don't leave anything out. These comprehensive lists include most possible items you could possibly want.

In this way, you'll become aware of your travel style in general and your clothing needs for this trip, and you will begin to form an idea of how much you want to take and what.

KNOW LOCAL CUSTOMS The way people dress them-selves and expect visitors to dress is key to your wardrobe. In some resort areas, an anything-goes dress code applies, whereas in others many restaurants frown on diners with bare feet or those wearing shorts, bathing suits, even T-shirts. Going abroad? Various countries maintain traditions of dress that differ from ours. In the Middle East, women need to dress modestly—no miniskirts, no trousers. Else-where, demure attire is similarly de rigueur to visit the sites you've traveled to see; if you want to visit St. Peter's in Rome or St. Mark's in Venice, for example, you can't wear shorts and your shoulders must be covered. Here, and in many other locations, a dignified look goes a long way—think skirts below the knee and shirts that are covered up—and forget about anything revealing or flashy. In some places, camouflage fabric is a no-go. In Europe, you may feel most comfortable in dark clothing—navy, black, gray, or dark brown, rather than splashy orange and fuchsia. In trop-ical areas, this kind of bright color feels right, and somber hues seem less appropriate.

Do check with the country's tourist office and consult a good guidebook. Especially if the weather will be hot when you visit, know the score about shorts—are short shorts okay, or must you stick with Bermudas, or skirts or trousers? What about capris for women? And what about sleeveless shirts or tank tops? Will bright colors make you stand out or fit right in? If you're visiting a resort, study the brochure and ask the concierge, the owner, or the reservationist.

HEED THE COMFORT FACTOR It goes without saying that you should never leave on a trip without well-broken-in shoes. It's all too easy to learn this the hard way, as footwear that felt supremely comfortable in the store develop strange friction points that leave your feet blistered and your sightseeing seriously curtailed.

Similarly, don't immediately run out and buy a whole new wardrobe. Because you will probably want to wear each item several times during your trip, you're better off with clothing you know you love, clothes that are comfortable and make you feel good. If you do end up buying something new, wear it a couple of times to make sure that you like it and to find out whether it's as wrinkleproof and easy to care for as you need your clothing to be on your trip.

(There is, of course, an exception to this general rule: socks. If your trip will involve a lot of walking, splurge on brand new socks, preferably performance socks in a cushiony, quick-drying, wicking fabric with a thickly padded bottom—check outdoors-oriented companies such as REI and L.L Bean. Old socks tend to be thin and have often lost their spring and, therefore, their cushioning properties. New socks will give your feet more staying power.)

EVALUATE YOUR TRAVEL STYLE When you travel, do you tend to be the person hauling a jumble pullman straining at its seams or are you the one who fits everything into one compact carry-on? Much depends on your personal attitude about your possessions. Do you like to travel light-through life? Are you an Oscar or a Felix about your handbag

RATIONALIZATIONS OF AN OVERPACKER

For some people, checking luggage is simply part of the trip—they are willing to put up with the hassle because they will be happier in the end. But are they, really?

"YOU NEVER KNOW WHAT YOU'RE GOING TO NEED" We've all heard this before, and many of us have said it ourselves. But times have changed. On our swiftly shrinking planet, 35mm film is now for sale in Kenyan villages. These days, if you haven't brought enough of something—or, heaven forbid, have forgotten a crucial item—chances are you'll be able to find it wherever you're going. Often, this can lead to pleasant discoveries. Bruce likes to shop for toiletries abroad. That's how he discovered he prefers English shaving cream over American brands. Susan began a lifelong love affair with honey soap in Nice, and Gregg makes a point of buying deodorant in each country he visits. He sees it as the first order of business in a new place—it lends a kind of wacky mission to his sightseeing.

"I WON'T HAVE ENOUGH DRESSY CLOTHING" The citizens of the world have all relaxed a lot over the last 20 years or so, with us jeaned-and-sneakered Americans leading the way. So why does an American going abroad feel the need to pull out all the stops? (If you've ever been to the London theater, you'll have noticed that all the dressed-up folks in tuxedos and furs in the front rows are package-tour Americans; the Brits themselves are in slacks and sweaters, up in the balcony.) Remember that you're a tourist; chances

or briefcase? Do your lifetime's mementoes fit into a shoe box, or could you fill an attic above a six-car garage with your acquisitions? If you are usually a pack rat, perhaps you are willing to do what it takes to have your possessions around you—or maybe you're ready to work toward a more streamlined travel style.

are, you're going to look, sound, and smell like a tourist no matter what you do. So you may as well be comfortable. Today, an understated ensemble in a dark color can take you everywhere. Black is always appropriate for evening, and it can be dressed up or down. A dark suit for men, or a simple jacket and tie, can do wonders.

"I'M NOT BUYING A THING" Let's be honest here: we'll take bets that you're going to buy a lot of things. And it's a safe bet that you'll want to wear what you buy even though you've packed more than enough to wear. Savvy travelers pack with these simple truisms in mind. Some even take along old clothing, buy new clothing, and leave their old duds in the hotel as a kind of reverse souvenir.

"THE BLUE FOR MONDAY, THE RED FOR TUESDAY . . ." Instead of packing extra outfits, fill in with accessories such as scarves, ties, and shirts. Accessories take up very little room and can dramatically change the personality of a basic outfit.

"JUST A FEW COMFORTS OF HOME . . ." Travelers who are daunted by leaving the familiar behind tend to over-pack. If you're among them, you need to pack a sense of adventure! Edna St. Vincent Millay once wrote, "There isn't a train I wouldn't take, no matter where it's going." Obviously a carry-on packer. Remember, no matter how much you try, you can't take it all with you. Plus, don't forget, it will be there when you return.

REMEMBER HOW YOU'LL GET THERE FROM HERE

If one thing serves to turn a pack rat into a minimalist, it's one or two experiences of lugging everything you've packed over long distances. So this is a good time to consider how you're getting to your destination and how you'll be getting around once you arrive there. Although it's never a good idea to over-pack, how much you take is less critical on trips when you're driving with your family and staying put at your destination than when an airplane is providing your transportation or you're moving around once you get there. If the latter, traveling light is even more important—especially if you're eschewing your own wheels for public transportation, as you might on a trip to Europe or Asia. If you'll need to walk substantial distances in cities with bumpy cobblestone sidewalks, you may end up carrying your suitcase, even if it has wheels.

CONSIDER CARRYING ON Although traveling lighter is always better, the question of how light is light enough looms especially large if you will be traveling by air. Airline rules become paramount, and they do vary from carrier to carrier, especially abroad. Knowing the regulations is vital. But even if you can travel heavy, you may not want to. Baggage slows you down at every step.

GO LIGHTLY IN EUROPE—OR ELSE

In some parts of Europe packing too much can entail painfully high overweight-baggage fees—and "too much" doesn't necessarily mean all that much. So check rules and limitations with each carrier on your itinerary—and pack for the most restrictive or be prepared to pay the price. (There's more leeway in the United States. Here "traveling heavy" simply means you will have to check your luggage. But even here, you won't check nine pieces of luggage without paying a pretty penny extra.)

If you pack light enough, you have the option of carrying all your luggage on board the plane. Then, if you breeze through airport security and want to take an earlier flight, you may be able to do so. Once you land, you can head into town right away, without waiting around at the baggage carousel or dealing with lost luggage. The freedom almost warrants the risk that delays might force you to lug your bags around the airport for a few hours—or even, in the event of reroutings, clear security with them multiple times (no mean feat nowadays).

WASHDAY BLUES? DON'T BE WEIGHED DOWN

How much you take is also a function of your position on laundry. You can pack fewer items if you don't mind doing laundry in your sink; if you view a self-service laundry as a way to experience your destination; or if you will be staying in one place long enough to have laundry or dry-cleaning done during your trip. You'll have to pack more if you'll be moving at a dead run for most of your journey, changing hotels every day—or if you don't trust the quality of the local laundries and dry-cleaners to handle the clothes you want to take. You don't want to hand over your vintage Chanel suit to just anyone.

HOW MUCH?

As a starting point, take at least two pairs of comfortable shoes; do your best to avoid taking more than three because shoes take up so much space. Limiting your shoe choices is especially tricky for women, given that different styles and lengths of skirts and trousers require completely different shoes. One answer: stick to just one basic wardrobe look. With this in mind, choose clothes that you can wear at least twice in a week—three times is better. When all your tops go with all your bottoms and all your bottoms work with all your shoes, mixing and matching can yield plenty of fresh looks; just add scarves and jewelry. Accordingly, for a week's trip, you should look smashing with three bottoms, four or five tops, a sweater, and a jacket that can be worn alone or over the sweater. Pack enough underwear and socks to last you between laundry; if yours come in a quick-dry fabric, three or four pairs should be plenty. Adjust further, depending on the style and purpose of the trip.

MAKE CLOTHES WORK HARD How many outfits can you make with each article of clothing? How versatile is each item? How often will you wear it? Try to have everything in your suitcase serve at least a couple of different purposes. For

BASIC WARDROBE OPTIONS FOR MEN

SUITS, JACKETS

- ❏ Blazer
- ❏ Sport coat
- ❏ Suits

TROUSERS

- ❏ Casual slacks
- ❏ Dress pants
- ❏ Jeans
- ❏ Shorts

SHIRTS

- ❏ Casual shirts
- ❏ Dress shirts
- ❏ Polo shirts
- ❏ T-shirts
- ❏ Turtlenecks

SWEATERS

- ❏ Cardigans
- ❏ Pullovers
- ❏ Sweater vest

ACCESSORIES

- ❏ Belts
- ❏ Cuff links
- ❏ Pocket squares
- ❏ Sunglasses
- ❏ Suspenders
- ❏ Ties

SHOES

- ❏ Boots
- ❏ Dress shoes
- ❏ Sandals
- ❏ Sneakers, athletic shoes
- ❏ Walking shoes
- ❏ Water shoes, thongs

SOCKS

- ❏ Athletic socks
- ❏ Dress socks

UNDERWEAR
- ❏ Boxers, briefs
- ❏ Long johns
- ❏ T-shirts

SLEEPWEAR
- ❏ Pajamas
- ❏ Robe
- ❏ Slippers

FOR SPORTS
- ❏ Bathing suits
- ❏ Sports equipment
- ❏ Swim goggles
- ❏ T-shirt or cover-up
- ❏ Workout gear

FOR EVENING
- ❏ Cuff links
- ❏ Cummerbund
- ❏ Dressy shoes

- ❏ Studs
- ❏ Tie
- ❏ Tux
- ❏ Tux shirt
- ❏ Vest

OUTERWEAR
- ❏ Baseball cap
- ❏ Gloves
- ❏ Overcoat
- ❏ Parka
- ❏ Raincoat, zip-out lining
- ❏ Scarf
- ❏ Sun hat
- ❏ Tote bag
- ❏ Umbrella
- ❏ Windbreaker
- ❏ Winter hat

this reason, women should focus on separates rather than dresses, although dresses may be necessary for certain occasions. Don't take an item you'll wear only once unless you absolutely can't live without it. And forget about having your suitcase give you the variety of your closet at home—one of the wonderful things about taking a trip is that you get away from all that.

Consider taking the time to try on every outfit you don't usually wear at home—shoes, bottom, top, sweater, jacket, accessories—to really ensure that all your outfits look and feel as good as you want them to.

Black trousers are the perfect multifunctional item; they can be dressed up or down, depending on what you put on top and on your feet. A navy or olive-green blazer looks great over jeans as well as business slacks. Long pants with zip-off legs that become shorts make an easy transition from walking-around-town to temple grounds are good to have on some trips. Leggings are good for working out, for wearing on the plane, and for lounging around your hotel room. A raincoat can keep you warm or you can use it as a robe. Large scarves lend style, polish, and warmth, and they're compact. A reversible jacket or wrap skirt can yield many looks as well.

THE RIGHT COLOR SCHEME One of the secrets of making items do double or triple or quadruple duty is to make a point of building your wardrobe around just two or three complementary colors, such as black, gray, and red; navy, red, and white; or brown, olive green, and cream. Doing this increases your outfit choices because everything goes together, so you'll get more mileage out of fewer pieces. Don't pair black with navy on the same trip. Each requires its own accessories, and they are not interchangeable. It bears repeating that dark colors don't show spots and soil— think black T-shirts rather than white ones (we all know that white T-shirts are magnets for spaghetti sauce). Less assertive than brights, dark colors are also more appropriate in many cities.

LOOK FOR LIGHTWEIGHT AND WRINKLEPROOF
As you evaluate your options and narrow your choices, go for items that are light in weight, wrinkle resistant, compact, and washable. A pair of thin jeans, perhaps made of Tencel, is preferable to the real thing, which take up a lot of space, even when ironed. Shorter, narrower skirts require fewer of your precious few cubic inches of suitcase space than longer, pleated, or flared ones.

Clothes made of fabric with built-in wrinkles tend to travel beautifully. Lightweight linen, although very cool, creases like crazy. If you like this rumpled look, you may consider packing linen; if you prefer to look crisp, leave your linens at home.

CONSIDER THE WRINKLE FACTOR

As you acquire new things for the trip, try this simple wrinkling test: Intentionally fold a piece of fabric between your fingers for a couple of minutes. If it refuses to crease, it will probably come out of your suitcase looking fresh as well.

ACCESSORIES—LESS IS MORE That old adage makes a lot of sense when it comes to traveling with jewelry. True, jewelry can really change the look of an outfit. On the other hand, when you're on the road, wearing good-looking jewelry (even rhinestones, plastic pearls, blue and green glass "emeralds" and "sapphires," and faux gold and silver) can be as good as posting a neon sign over your head that reads ROB ME. Besides, the more you take with you, the greater your chance of mislaying something by accident.

Most important, don't pack what you don't want to lose— choose a few simple pieces that blend with everything and that you can wear all together without looking like Mr. T. Ethnic earrings and arty necklaces will often work, although on some trips, truth be told, you really do need your pearls. If you must bring more jewelry than you can wear all at once, carry it on your person or pack it in your carry-on bag. Always leave what you're not wearing in your hotel safe deposit box. And don't take anything off without putting it away immediately—to take it off is to risk leaving it behind on the sink or the bedside table, where it may be lost forever.

EDIT YOUR CLOTHING LIST As you weigh these many factors, along with your daily itinerary, a clothing list will evolve. Study it carefully. Notice how many times you've listed a specific item—shorts, for instance, or T-shirts. Do you have shorts listed seven times for your seven-day trip? In that case, you'll probably be able to make do with only two or three pairs, as long as one is black, brown, or another color that doesn't show dirt. Have you listed your lime-green Manolo Blahnik pumps just once? Better to leave them at home in favor of a more versatile pair of shoes. Here, right here, is where your clothing editing begins, when you can consider all the variables calmly. It certainly beats gazing, panic-stricken, into the yawning mouth of your suitcase the evening before your 7 AM flight.

SOME ADDITIONAL GENERAL THOUGHTS If you'll be traveling outside the United States, stay away from logo T-shirts, sneakers, baseball hats, and jogging suits, which immediately label you as an American, for better or for worse. On the other hand, if you're going to Walt Disney World or another theme park, wearing the logos of hometown teams and favorite companies can spark conversations with your fellow travelers, people who are waiting in the same lines that you are, when any conversation can make the time pass more quickly.

Pockets are always useful, but especially when you're traveling.

If you must indulge the occasional urge to bring something totally impractical, err on the side of the compact. Items that take little suitcase space but make a big statement are definitely worth their weight. Toss in a silky sleeveless knit top or scarf with a bit of shine and you can instantly glamorize the dark skirt or trousers you wore for sightseeing all day.

PLAN YOUR INFLIGHT OUTFIT Once you've pared down your list, choose travel clothing for yourself, composed of items already noted. It makes sense to wear the heaviest, bulkiest items on your list—you'll automatically have less to pack. If you are flying, wear neat-looking, loose-fitting clothing—loose-fitting because your body swells in flight. (Air inside your body, which is pressurized at the altitude of your departure city, expands as you ascend—remember your middle-school science class?)

Some men traveling directly from the airport to a business meeting wear a dress shirt, suit jacket, and comfortable pants, bringing suit pants and a tie in a carry-on bag and changing on the aircraft or just after landing. Women on business trips can duck into the lavatory to take off their traveling clothes—say, slacks with a comfortable elasticized waist—and put on a slim skirt or crisp slacks and dressier shoes.

WHAT TO WEAR ON THE PLANE

- ❑ Your bulkiest clothes and shoes
- ❑ A sweater or other cover-up
- ❑ Something nice if you want an upgrade
- ❑ Loose clothing in soft, natural fibers
- ❑ Low-heeled leather or canvas slip-on shoes
- ❑ Warm socks

FOLLOW THE WEATHER Start checking the temperatures for your destination a week before your trip. Having up-to-date weather information allows you to revise your packing list appropriately and also to consider buying sunscreen, insect repellent, long johns, or whatever else you may need for the weather. For all the wrong reasons, you would always remember the London vacation full of snow and cold that you had to weather clad only in a thin raincoat because you took off expecting London's typically mild weather—only to experience one of the worst winters in British history. Or the trip to New York's Finger Lakes, when you drove straight into a blizzard—in your thin white Keds. (The boots you bought at the first available shoe store still remind you of that mess.)

As you think about the weather, be sure to consider the humidity level, because Manhattan scorchers—or anywhere else where it's not only 95° but also humid—feel completely different than the same temperature in Phoenix, where the air is dry.

PACK YOUR RATTIEST CLOTHING OR YOUR FAVORITES?

Among the Fodor's readership there are two schools of thought. Some travelers hand-select a few beloved items for their trip and leave the rest at home. Others pack their rattiest underwear, the pretty shirt with the ink stain that can be worn only underneath a sweater, or other similarly damaged goods—and during their trips carefully deposit worn items in the trash or give them away and perhaps even buy new clothing en route. Brilliant or brainless? You be the judge. But if you plan on shopping in Asia, remember that larger American sizes simply aren't available, and, unless you're tiny, you'll have to do without or take the time to have your replacement wardrobe custom-made.

THE MULTICLIMATE TRIP If your itinerary will take you through several climatic zones, it's smart to start your journey in colder areas if you have the option. Then you can ship your cold-weather gear home as soon as you head for warmth. Otherwise, try to plan a wardrobe full of layers, so that you can pile clothes on, or peel them off, as temperatures warrant. Lightweight and so compact that they use up virtually no suitcase space, silk long johns are a great base layer. A turtleneck, shirt, sweater, or fleece sweatshirt, and lightweight nylon or Gore-Tex shell will take you through a variety of situations. A hat, perhaps a wool beret or a fleece cap, adds still more warmth. Ditto for a fleece neck gaiter. And only the fleece sweatshirt is bulky.

When it's cold at home and you're flying to a warm destination, leave your heavy coat behind; you may be able to lock it in your car's trunk if leaving your car at the airport. Or leave it all at home, and have the person picking you up at the airport bring your coat. Or wear compact layers—such as silk long johns, sweater, light jacket, scarf, hat, and gloves—and then strip them off on the plane and stuff them into your tote bag.

If it's warm where you live and you're bound for cold weather, put layers into your tote and change on the plane. Or send your coat ahead.

IN CASE OF RAIN If rain is in the offing, as in cold, wet rain of the type that you often encounter in Britain and Ireland or in New York City in late fall and winter, don't leave home without waterproofing your shoes with a good silicone spray. If you do accidentally put your foot into an ankle-deep puddle, loosely crumple up a page from the New York Times or the Guardian or the Herald Tribune, and stuff. This will help your shoes dry a little faster.

Know-How for Trips of All Kinds

The tips on the next few pages should help you further define your wardrobe (and your gear) based on your type of trip. Edit our lists for your own trip. And remember that at least one outfit won't go in your suitcase but will be worn in transit.

BASIC WARDROBE OPTIONS FOR WOMEN

BUSINESS WEAR

- ❏ Dresses
- ❏ Suits

JACKETS

- ❏ Blazer
- ❏ Other jackets

TROUSERS

- ❏ Casual slacks
- ❏ Dress pants
- ❏ Jeans
- ❏ Shorts
- ❏ Leggings

SKIRTS

- ❏ Casual skirts
- ❏ Dress skirts

SHIRTS

- ❏ Blouses
- ❏ Casual shirts
- ❏ Knit tops
- ❏ Polo shirts
- ❏ T-shirts
- ❏ Turtlenecks

DRESSES

- ❏ Casual dresses
- ❏ Sundresses

SWEATERS

- ❏ Cardigans
- ❏ Pullovers
- ❏ Sweater vest

ACCESSORIES

- ❏ Belts
- ❏ Cuff links
- ❏ Earrings, necklaces
- ❏ Hair ties, barrettes
- ❏ Handbag
- ❏ Pareo, sarong
- ❏ Scarves
- ❏ Sunglasses

SHOES

- ❏ Boots
- ❏ Dress pumps
- ❏ Flats
- ❏ Walking shoes
- ❏ Sandals

- ❑ Sneakers, athletic shoes
- ❑ Water shoes, thongs

SOCKS

- ❑ Athletic socks
- ❑ Knee socks
- ❑ Panty hose
- ❑ Trouser socks

LINGERIE

- ❑ Bras
- ❑ Camisoles
- ❑ Long johns
- ❑ Panties
- ❑ Slips
- ❑ Sports bras
- ❑ Support garments

SLEEPWEAR

- ❑ Nightwear
- ❑ Robe
- ❑ Slippers

FOR SPORTS

- ❑ Bathing suits
- ❑ Bathing suit cover-up

- ❑ Sports equipment
- ❑ Swim goggles
- ❑ Workout gear

FOR EVENING

- ❑ Dress, gown, or suit
- ❑ Evening bag
- ❑ Evening wrap, shawl
- ❑ Jewelry
- ❑ Lingerie
- ❑ Stockings

OUTERWEAR

- ❑ Baseball cap
- ❑ Gloves
- ❑ Overcoat
- ❑ Parka
- ❑ Raincoat, zip-out lining
- ❑ Sun hat
- ❑ Tote bag
- ❑ Umbrella
- ❑ Windbreaker
- ❑ Winter hat

▶ Active Trips and Adventures

On these trips, you may be carrying everything, so you may need to pack for portability. Most likely, your clothing should be unfussy and durable—style will be secondary to comfort.

If you are going with an adventure travel outfitter, you will probably be sent a packing list before the trip. Often, the staff members of these businesses are adventure lovers themselves who really know what works in the environment you'll be exploring. Don't be shy about calling to ask for advice on name brands and specific articles of clothing. Be sure to ask about laundry facilities; on some Africa safaris, outfitters encourage you to pack light by offering overnight service.

When assembling your wardrobe, remember that you'll want to dress in layers that can be put on and taken off as the temperature and your activity level dictate. This is true whether you're traveling in the mountains, the tropics, or the desert. A poncho serves many purposes. Garments made of fleece such as Polartec, Polarfleece, and other microfibers are warm, lightweight, and easy to pack. Fleece items can be compressed using special vacuum bags available from accessories sections of housewares stores and travel goods stores.

For a river-rafting trip, get a neoprene eyewear retainer to hold your glasses securely onto your head; Croakies were the first of these straps but there are others. Quick-drying fabrics such as Supplex and fleece, which has the additional virtue of keeping you warm even when it's wet, are most comfortable.

Most important is a good pair of shoes. Know your chosen terrain before you go. And make sure to break in new boots.

Adventure trips require a more complete first-aid kit than the one suggested in Chapter 3. Compact yet fully stocked kits are available at sports retail stores.

ABOUT YOUR LUGGAGE A trip in the great outdoors requires rugged luggage that can take a beating from the elements. In these circumstances, waterproofing is critical—

think of a river-rafting trip, or imagine your bags being strapped to the top of a safari bus during a storm. Then, too, you'll need pieces that allow you to pack a minimum amount of stuff with the most portability. Duffels and travel packs really answer the call for situations like this. Both provide enough protection for the type of clothing you'll pack.

IDEAS FOR YOUR DAY PACK

- ❏ Binoculars
- ❏ Camera, film
- ❏ Compass
- ❏ Extra clothing
- ❏ First-aid kit
- ❏ Flashlight
- ❏ Insect repellent
- ❏ Lip balm
- ❏ Map
- ❏ Matches
- ❏ Pocket knife
- ❏ Snacks
- ❏ Sunglasses
- ❏ Sunscreen
- ❏ Water bottle, filled

A day pack is essential on many kinds of adventure trips. In it, you'll want to store extra clothing appropriate for the weather and the climate: a bathing suit, an extra T-shirt, a waterproof parka, mittens and a hat, and a spare pair of socks. A small flashlight can come in handy: check the bulb and batteries and replace them if necessary. Depending on the nature of your trip, you may also want to include signaling devices such as flares or a whistle.

▶ Active Trips in Hot Weather

Loose-fitting and light-colored clothing is the way to go. Shirts with long sleeves and long pants minimize sun exposure. Natural fibers such as cotton or silk are coolest, along with cottonlike performance synthetics such as Supplex or CoolMax, which wick moisture away from your body and dry quickly. Your strategy should be to bring as little as possible, so you aren't weighed down by your bags.

CHECK LOCAL CUSTOMS Know the score about tank tops and shorts—sometimes they simply are not acceptable. Some package safari trips have an occasional dress-up evening; sequins and dinner jackets are not necessary, but a long skirt or sundress for women and khakis and a casual shirt for men are appropriate. If you do bring makeup, remember that lipstick can melt in the heat; pack lip pencils instead. For the same reason, have prescription medications dispensed as tablets if possible, rather than as capsules. And don't forget a sun hat, sunscreen, and insect repellent.

KEEP COOL An old-fashioned folding fan is nice to have when it's steamy. A bandanna wards off dust and is useful to mop off your forehead when it's sweaty.

TEND YOUR FEET This is especially important in hot weather and hot climates. Shoes that allow your feet to breathe, such as sport sandals, are essential on the beach. In a rain forest or jungle, quick-drying socks and sturdy closed-toe shoes are mandatory as protection from insects and water-borne bacteria—consider lightweight hiking shoes made of canvas or open-weave nylon. In the desert, you need sturdy hiking boots to shield your feet from rocks underfoot. For added foot relief, pack a tiny bottle of foot powder or a one-ounce bottle of witch hazel as a midafternoon pick-me-up.

BE PREPARED Rain gear is always useful. Even in the desert there are occasional sudden downpours, and your anorak will be welcome during windstorms, particularly if it's made of breathable fabric. The sudden plummeting of temperatures when the sun goes down will send you straight to your tent in search of a sweater.

KEEP ESSENTIALS COOL If you're making short day hikes, you may want to pack a lightweight cooler and synthetic ice to keep film or drinks from getting overly warm.

DIVING? If you'll be snorkeling or scuba diving, be sure to bring any dive equipment that you particularly care about. You may feel more comfortable with your own regulator, your own fins, and your own prescription-lens face mask, for instance. Bring your own dive tables, your dive watch, and your diver certification card as well.

BRING THE RIGHT CAMERA Finally, whether you're diving or desert-bound, consider an underwater camera with tightly fitting gaskets. In the desert you need it because it's so dusty, and dust seeps into every crevice of a regular point-and-shoot or 35mm single-lens-reflex camera and potentially jams it up.

IDEAS FOR HOT WEATHER

- ❏ Anorak
- ❏ Bandanna
- ❏ Cooler
- ❏ Day pack
- ❏ Dive tables
- ❏ Diver certification card
- ❏ Diving equipment
- ❏ Film
- ❏ Folding fan
- ❏ Hiking boots
- ❏ Lip pencils
- ❏ Insect repellent
- ❏ Medication in tablet form
- ❏ Snorkeling equipment
- ❏ Socks
- ❏ Sport sandals
- ❏ Sun hat
- ❏ Synthetic ice
- ❏ Umbrella
- ❏ Underwater camera

FOR THE DESERT

- ❏ Sweater or jacket
- ❏ Dustproof camera case

FOR THE TROPICS

- ❏ Antifungal foot powder

▶ Active Vacations in Winter

Elliot, a lawyer, has some advice to people considering traveling in winter: Don't. He thinks that bulky clothing translates into a packing nightmare.

Not necessarily.

THINK LAYERS Remember the principle of dressing in layers. Next to your skin, wear long johns made of silk or a moisture-wicking synthetic—both leggings and a crewneck or turtleneck. On top of that should go T-shirts, turtlenecks, or long-sleeve shirts. Top it all off with a sweater or fleece pullover, depending on the temperature; followed by your snowsuit, ski parka, or windbreaker, and your snow pants (compressed using vacuum bags, if necessary).

STAY TOASTY FROM HEAD TO TOE Remember the old saying, "If your feet are cold, put on a hat"? To the hat you should add a warm fleece neck gaiter. On your feet, go with whatever is state-of-the-art in ski socks at the time of your trip. They should retain their insulating properties even when they're wet—do recognize that they may get wet, and bring several pairs. (If they are of a quick-drying material, so much the better, though if you're staying in a condo with laundry facilities, this is less of a concern.) You'll need your socks to fit underneath your ski boots or hiking boots as well as under your après-sport footwear. And when you're skiing, if all else fails, pick up one of those little hand- or foot-warming packets in the base lodge and experience instant, miraculous warmth.

SOME EXTRAS ARE WORTH PACKING You should also bring sunscreen and lip balm to protect against snow-reflected sun- and windburn. If your parka pockets aren't commodious, bring a fanny pack to stash this, your camera, extra film, and any other necessities, such as a pocket-size pack of tissues for blowing your nose or defogging your goggles or glasses.

SLOW IT DOWN

If you're bringing film to the beach or to snow country, buy a relatively slow speed, since sun on both snow and sand can generate a lot of light.

Walkie-talkies are fun to use when your family splits up into smaller groups. Just don't forget the chargers and adapters and voltage converters for the chargers if you're headed outside the United States.

OFF THE SLOPES If you're taking a ski or snowboarding vacation, don't forget to include warm clothing that will take you out to a nice dinner après-ski, including footwear for indoors and out with appropriate socks, driving gloves, a neck scarf, and a hat to wear between your lodging place and your dinner destination, and a layered outfit that won't leave you shivering while your car warms up. You may end up wearing long johns during every waking hour.

SHIP OR CHECK? As for your equipment, some skiers and boarders send their boards, skis, and poles to their resort via overnight courier—it saves hassles at the airport. If you're flying and your feet are hard to fit, consider carrying your boots on board the plane; if they were lost in transit, your vacation could be vastly less pleasurable.

Do invest in bags for your boards, skis, and boots. Some have enough room to pack a few extra garments, and they protect your equipment from road salt when you drive between the airport or your home and your ski destination.

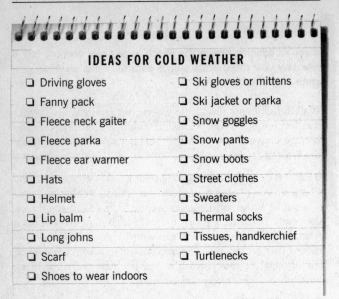

IDEAS FOR COLD WEATHER

- ❏ Driving gloves
- ❏ Fanny pack
- ❏ Fleece neck gaiter
- ❏ Fleece parka
- ❏ Fleece ear warmer
- ❏ Hats
- ❏ Helmet
- ❏ Lip balm
- ❏ Long johns
- ❏ Scarf
- ❏ Shoes to wear indoors
- ❏ Ski gloves or mittens
- ❏ Ski jacket or parka
- ❏ Snow goggles
- ❏ Snow pants
- ❏ Snow boots
- ❏ Street clothes
- ❏ Sweaters
- ❏ Thermal socks
- ❏ Tissues, handkerchief
- ❏ Turtlenecks

▶ In the Mountains

On these you'll often pass through a series of microclimates in one afternoon; as soon as you get heated up through exertion, you can bet the temperature will fall. So make sure you have lots of layers, which you can lay on and peel off as temperatures dictate. In early spring and fall, when it's still chilly, start with synthetic underwear, next to your skin, the kind that wicks moisture away from your body (bring several sets). In warmer weather, wear quick-drying shorts or pants. (You'll want several sets of these, too.) You may then want a T-shirt or turtleneck, topped by a fleece vest and/or pullover and a windbreaker made of material that's waterproof yet breathable, such as Gore-Tex. In spring or fall, just in case, you may want to throw a hat and a fleece neck gaiter into your day pack, along with your water bottle and some high-energy trail snacks such as raisins, nuts, and chocolate. On your feet, you'll want socks with good cushioning properties to wear

When you pack your MCI Calling Card, it's like packing your loved ones along too.

Your MCI Calling Card is the easy way to stay in touch when you travel. Use it to call to and from over 125 countries. Plus, every time you call, you can earn frequent flier miles. So wherever your travels take you, call home with your MCI Calling Card. It's even easy to get one. Just visit **www.mci.com/worldphone** or **www.mci.com/partners**.

EASY TO CALL WORLDWIDE

1. Just enter the WorldPhone® access number of the country you're calling from.

2. Enter or give the operator your MCI Calling Card number.

3. Enter or give the number you're calling.

Argentina	0-800-222-6249
Bermuda ÷	1-800-888-8000
Brazil	0800-890-0012
United States	1-800-888-8000

÷ Limited availability.

EARN FREQUENT FLIER MILES

Find America *with a Compass*

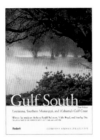

Written by local authors and illustrated throughout
with spectacular color images, the Compass American
Guides reveal the character and culture of more than
40 of America's most fascinating destinations. Perfect
for residents who want to explore their own backyard,
and visitors who want an insider's perspective on
the history, heritage, and all there is to see and do.

Fodor's COMPASS AMERICAN GUIDES

At bookstores everywhere.

over wicking liner socks. And don't forget your camera. If your venture into the hills calls for river rafting or other watery activities, you may want to go shopping for a camera that can handle more than the occasional splash.

Finally, if your trip calls for a return to civilization (or in case you'll be day hiking and returning to a cozy ranch or bed-and-breakfast at the end of every day), be sure to include street clothes, including shoes and socks. If you have any thoughts of a nice dinner out during your trip or at either end, plan accordingly.

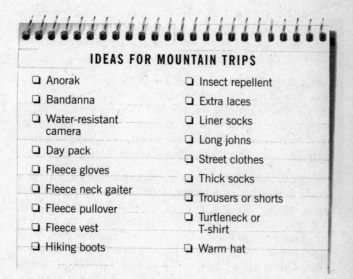

IDEAS FOR MOUNTAIN TRIPS

- ❏ Anorak
- ❏ Bandanna
- ❏ Water-resistant camera
- ❏ Day pack
- ❏ Fleece gloves
- ❏ Fleece neck gaiter
- ❏ Fleece pullover
- ❏ Fleece vest
- ❏ Hiking boots
- ❏ Insect repellent
- ❏ Extra laces
- ❏ Liner socks
- ❏ Long johns
- ❏ Street clothes
- ❏ Thick socks
- ❏ Trousers or shorts
- ❏ Turtleneck or T-shirt
- ❏ Warm hat

▶ Business Trips and Seminars

Whether it's a convention, a conference, a trade show, a sales call, an interview, or a high-level brainstorming session, you're traveling for business, not pleasure. Striking the right professional appearance can help you careerwise, so pack thoughtfully.

KNOW THE ROPES Choose conservative suits or casual professional clothing, depending on the customs of your field of business and the business activities you anticipate (roll-up-the-sleeves seminars as opposed to client presentations, for example). Find out the local business customs for the city you're going to. The open-collar shirt that's appropriate in Singapore will cost you points in London.

Meeting new people? Err on the side of the conservative—a loud tie or low-cut blouse could create a disastrous first impression.

HOW TO PACK LESS Look over your itinerary to decide whether you will meet different people (fresh sales prospects, perhaps) each day or see the same colleagues over and over. This will dictate the number of outfits you'll need.

On a short trip, men may be able to get by with one suit—just change the color of your shirt and tie each day. If you're dressing more casually, you can pair a single sweater or blazer with different pants or skirts and shirts each day. Opt for an unobtrusive style, and chances are that your clients or associates won't focus on the fact that you're repeating the outfit.

But some things are worth the extra space. If you'll be at a trade show, where you have to look good while standing on your feet all day, a change of shoes is welcome halfway through the day. (A fresh pair of socks will also do wonders as a pick-me-up.) Because accidents will happen, pack extra pairs of panty hose and one or two extra shirts or blouses—one of them might be ever-forgiving black. If you should spill coffee all over yourself, you will be thrilled to have the extra item. And, on the subject of the unanticipated, you may find it worth your while to tuck in a compact folding umbrella.

PLAN FOR DOWNTIME Women may want to pack one dressy outfit as well, especially if their business attire is very conservative. Men can still get by with a daytime suit at dinner, unless a black-tie event is on the agenda.

Bring some smart casual clothing if you'll be with colleagues rather than on your own after work. This can be valuable bonding time that will enhance your working relationships, and remaining in a suit may make you seem standoffish.

Don't forget to toss in something to wear when hanging around in your room—perhaps a big T-shirt and leggings or a silk robe, which packs very compactly.

In fall and spring, anticipate a change in the weather. Throw in a silk undershirt, silk-lined leather gloves, a wool or silk neck scarf, a lightweight hat, and thin wool socks—all of which will help warm you up without weighing you down.

FITNESS TO GO Just because you're traveling on business doesn't mean you can't exercise; in fact, it may help you de-stress. Most hotels have pools, exercise rooms, or both, so pack your swimsuit or a pair of shorts and T-shirt and your sneakers.

You can also plan to work out in your room. Easy-to-pack equipment for a hotel-room workout might include a Walk-man with energizing tapes, industrial-size rubber bands for resistance exercises, inflatable bags or empty plastic bottles to fill with water and use as hand weights, or a jump rope.

Most exercise clothing is made of fabric that dries quickly, so if you have packed some liquid detergent, you can bring one set of clothing and wash it after each use.

DON'T FORGET YOUR FEET If you're heading to a meeting or trade show where you'll be standing for hours at a time, make sure the shoes you bring are comfortable—flats are a good idea for women. One woman executive advises packing a pair of slippers, which she puts on after a day in the exhibit hall.

A bit of astringent will refresh your feet after a hot soak.

ABOUT YOUR LUGGAGE Business travelers find that garment bags and wheeled pullmans are most convenient for their needs. They do the best job protecting formal clothing,

and the pieces add their own bit of polish to your appearance,
allowing you to look organized and professional.

For women, pair a briefcase and small handbag rather than a
larger tote bag; you can tuck the purse into the briefcase to
get through the airport and onto the plane, and take just the
purse with you when you step out for dinner.

▶ Casual Vacations

Casual vacations, such as a weekend trip to a bed-and-breakfast or a quaint small hotel in the country, require clothing
suited to your activities.

GOLF OR TENNIS, ANYONE? If sports such as golf and
tennis are available, bring appropriate clothes and footwear;
call ahead to see if you can rent equipment at your destination. (You'll want to call ahead anyway to reserve tee times or
court times.)

COUNTRY WALKS OR LEISURELY PEDALING? If
hitting the trails is on your to-do list, be sure you've got the
right shoes. And if you're going into tall grass or woods in tick
country—for bird-watching, perhaps—be sure to pack long
pants, socks, and long-sleeve shirts.

If you're bike touring, don't forget your helmet and bike clothing. Be sure to include at least one waterproof layer and a thermal layer underneath if the weather's likely to get cold.
Depending on when and where you plan to cycle, you may
want to acquire a light for night riding, spare tire tubes and a
patch kit, cycling gloves, and a water bottle if you don't already
have them. Ditto for a good lock—you will need to leave your
bike at some point, if only to go inside a store to replenish your
drink supply. Even if you're carrying all your gear on your bike,
consider bringing at least one set of street clothes and a pair of
regular shoes so that you can go out to dinner without looking
like a straggler from the Tour de France.

HORSING AROUND? For horseback riding, toss in jeans and shoes with heels—or, if you have them, your jodhpurs, helmet, and riding boots. Helmets and boots take up a lot of luggage room; they're musts even if you're not a serious rider.

GOING ANTIQUING? Stay away from long, sweeping skirts, wide-brimmed hats, and bulky jackets, which can wreak havoc in narrow-aisled shops full of expensive breakables. You'll probably have large items shipped home, but toss some bubble wrap in your luggage when you pack, and leave room in your carry-on for small items, safely swaddled.

EATING OUT? On a weekend trip, you'll need fewer clothes for fewer days, so pruning your wardrobe is less of a problem. If you plan to be out sightseeing and playing sports by day, it may be worth it to bring a change of clothes for dinner each night. It'll make dinner out seem more of a treat and will give you the illusion of a longer, fuller, yet more relaxed day.

When researching your trip, find out if there's a superb restaurant in the area that you'd like to try. Call ahead for reservations, and pack at least one dressy outfit for the big night.

PLAN ON PICNICS Bring a soft cooler from home; slip in plastic forks and spoons, some paper plates and paper napkins, and a bottle opener. Add a corkscrew and a knife if you're driving or checking your luggage. If weight isn't an issue, bring a sheet or blanket to sit on.

THE RIGHT JACKET Spring, fall, or summer, a windbreaker is handy. Look for one that's waterproof, has lots of pockets, and can be rolled into a tiny pouch. In winter, a fleece pullover serves the same purpose. Not only does a light jacket bridge all sorts of weather changes, but the pockets are handy for carrying odds and ends, including a camera, wallet, map, guidebook, and water bottle. For short excursions you may be able to do without a day pack or purse if you've got a big front pouch in your jacket.

HERE'S A GOOD EXCUSE TO PACK MORE Casual trips are often car trips—so you can haul more stuff, even leaving some locked in your trunk overnight if you're changing hotels each day. This allows you to include more of everything, including sports gear—snowshoes as well as skis, for example, or snorkels and fins as well as a beach umbrella. Just don't get the car so loaded down that there's no room for you.

ABOUT YOUR LUGGAGE For a quick casual vacation, opt for a suitcase with wheels or a duffel bag, depending on how you prefer to carry your luggage. Both provide adequate protection for sporty casual clothing, and the duffel can take one or two fancier garments without creasing chaos. Choose a bag on the small side, since you often have to carry your own bags at B&Bs. Also consider bringing a lightweight duffel for sports gear.

▶ City Vacations

Cities are inherently more formal than resorts or rural areas, but unless you're there on business, your style can be relatively casual. Remember above all that cities have stores; shopping may in fact be part of your itinerary. Anything you decide not to pack can be bought later at your destination.

BE KIND TO YOUR TOOTSIES Sightseeing usually requires lots of walking on pavement; in Europe this often means cobblestones. A pair of sturdy, comfortable, low-heeled shoes is a must. Stay away from sandals, which let your feet get grimy and don't protect your toes. To make shoes do double duty, men may want to take brogues or loafers, which are comfortable for walking yet look presentable when paired with a suit or sport jacket.

Bring extra socks, preferably in quick-dry yarns that you can wash out every day. There's nothing like a change of socks in late afternoon to cajole a few more miles out of tired feet.

SAY CHEESE! Speaking of sightseeing—it usually requires a camera. Don't forget it.

KNOW LOCAL DO'S AND TABOOS Get acquainted with your destination city's customs and traditions. Milan may be the Italian design capital, but women are still expected to cover their bare shoulders with a scarf when entering the city's famous cathedral.

However, you needn't dress as formally as you might expect. After all, you're a tourist. So even though businesspeople in the same city wear suits, shorts are perfectly okay for summer sightseeing in many areas—but again, check your guidebook to ascertain local customs.

LAYER, LAYER, LAYER If you're the sort who likes to be out and about all day, anticipate changes in temperature. On her summer trip to San Francisco, Wendy was very glad she'd brought light jackets for herself and her boys—they needed them in the chilly morning fog and after dinner, even though afternoon highs were in the 70s. Even where the weather is uniformly warm, remember that indoor museums and shopping malls may be frigidly air-conditioned.

PLAN FOR AFTER DARK Keep in mind what you'll be doing at night. If you'll be attending evening performances of the opera or ballet, or sampling an elegant restaurant, include one more dressy outfit. One should be enough, though, if you won't be seeing the same people night after night.

BRING AN UMBRELLA Observe the Boy Scouts' motto, and be prepared!

PRECAUTIONS Women should wear a minimum of jewelry. Flashy finery only attracts trouble even if it's just costume jewelry—outsiders may think it's real. And even if you don't normally wear a money belt or security pouch, you should consider doing so in cities.

ABOUT YOUR LUGGAGE For your urban vacation, you might wish to mix and match your luggage. Take a lightweight garment bag for a few dressy outfits and a small suitcase with wheels for the rest of your gear.

▶ Cruises

A cruise vacation requires several types of clothing and perhaps a bit more of it than other trips. That's fine, because after you've unpacked, you won't even see your bags again until it's time to disembark. Most cruise lines issue an exhaustive list of suggested clothing for your time on board and ashore.

FOR SHORE EXCURSIONS Bring casual, sporty clothing with a conservative slant for shore excursions—leave tank tops and miniskirts on the ship. Layers are always a good idea. For an Alaska cruise, layers are the thing, but a good windbreaker, hat, and gloves are a must, even in August. You'll also be glad to have a water bottle that you can slip into your day pack.

Good walking shoes, broken in before the trip, are best for shore excursions, whether you'll be strolling on cobblestones or clambering over ruins.

For all climates, you'll need a sun hat or other head covering, because you don't want to be forced to waste your brief time in port on a midday siesta in the shade. Bring a couple of good books; you can't count on finding something you want to read, although many ships do have good libraries. And don't forget your camera and film—and a compact folding umbrella, just in case.

SWIMMING AND SPORTS Pack sunscreen, bathing suits, and a cover-up (perhaps a pareo or sarong) for the sundeck and pool; you may want to add a bathing cap, since some ships' pools are saltwater, which can be hard on sensitive hair. Include workout wear if you plan to keep up your fitness program or take advantage of the ship's exercise facilities and spa. And bring sports equipment if your cruise's scheduled port stops allow access to tennis courts and golf courses.

AFTER DARK The cruise line's suggested clothing list will spell out how many formal nights to expect. For a typical weeklong cruise, you can count on at least two. For these evenings, women are expected to wear an evening dress, men a dark suit or tuxedo. Break out the sequins and taffeta—a cruise may be the one time you can wear that bridesmaid's dress again.

The theme evenings scheduled by some cruises are more fun if you get into the spirit. Find out what's planned for your cruise and pack something to go with it—berets for French night or Hawaiian shirts for a Polynesian evening, for example.

On most other evenings, dress is semiformal, which means a dress or pants suit for women or a sport jacket, tie, and slacks for men. Casual evenings, generally the first and last nights on board, call for neat-looking street clothes. Most ships do not permit shorts at dinner in the formal dining room, and jeans may or may not be okay; it varies from ship to ship.

Women should bring a shawl or other light wrap to wear in air-conditioned rooms and for after-dinner stargazing on deck. It's also a good idea to bring plenty of panty hose, since you may not be able to find the size you need in shipboard shops.

ELECTRICALS Here's another thing to look into before you get too deep into your packing. Bringing an iron, hair dryer, or electric curling iron may or may not be an option. Find out whether they're permitted and whether you'll need a voltage converter and adapter plugs.

PRECAUTIONS Lest seasickness strike, consider packing Sea Bands, which use acupressure to quiet an unsettled stomach. In many ports, local thieves and pickpockets consider cruise passengers prime game. Safeguard your valuables. Don't flaunt money, your passport, expensive camera equipment, or jewelry.

ABOUT YOUR LUGGAGE Pack formal clothing in a garment bag and the rest in a suitcase or duffel. Take along a day pack for shore excursions—it's helpful for toting water, an extra sweater, a camera, and film, among other essentials.

▶ Family Vacations

Depending on your children's ages, you may wish to include them in the packing process by encouraging them to bring you what they consider to be appropriate clothing and toys. (Happy camper tip: try not to laugh in front of the kids.) Or you may wish to spend some quality time with each of them and supervise their choices, remembering that asking your children to help can backfire. "If I let them choose," says Donna of her children, "they forget something important, like socks. Sometimes, it's a guessing game. If I don't pack what I know they'll want even though they've forgotten it, they'll wind up blaming Mommy. So if everyone is to be happy—including me—I find it's easier simply to pack for them." Michael, father of two, agrees. "If my children choose a relatively new toy, I always pack a tried-and-true one as well," he says. "Nine times out of ten, they want the comfort of the old one, and are they glad to find it waiting for them!"

TOUGH TEENS The packing situation gets exponentially pricklier with teenagers. Theoretically, a teenager ought to be able to handle this job, and if you've got kids this age you know how they resent parental involvement. Still, their judgment may not always be totally reliable. ("Mom, I'll die rather than wear that flowered dress. You know I like my overalls better, and I'm sure no one at the wedding will care.") A good middle road may be to review their packing list ahead of time, making tactful suggestions. Or just inspect the suitcase once it's packed when your teen isn't around to protest.

THE DIAPER CONUNDRUM If your son or daughter is young, and still in diapers, one tough question is perennial: do you bring a whole trip's supply of disposable diapers or buy them when you get there?

Buying diapers shouldn't be a problem in the United States, although if you're arriving late in the day, you'll need enough to last until morning—the last thing you want to do on arrival is peel around town looking for Pampers. If you're heading for a resort, however, it may be hard to get off-site, and the resort shops won't necessarily sell diapers, or diapers in the size you need or at a price you consider acceptable to pay. (One mother recalls forking over $1.25 per diaper at a California resort.)

If you're leaving the United States, bringing your own diapers isn't such a bad idea. In the Caribbean, disposable diapers are very expensive; in Europe, prices aren't bad, but stores may stock only local brands, or the size you need may not be available. For instance, French mothers toilet train their youngsters early, so junior sizes in disposables are hard to come by. (Most Fodor's guidebooks include this kind of information.)

It all depends on the length of your trip. For a short beach vacation, take the diapers and disposable swim diapers you think you'll need. (If portability is really crucial, you could always invest in an old-fashioned washable swim diaper to cut down on how many you'll use.) For a two-week jaunt to Europe, take enough diapers to get through the first week, to buy yourself some time before you have to go diaper-hunting. If on Day Two, you happen into a *supermercado* that sells Les Pampers at a decent price, all the better. If this is the plan, make sure you know your baby's weight in kilos, which is how diaper sizes are expressed throughout the metric world. And do research your destination's diaper scene before you count on being able to buy what you need. Another option is to mail your favorite diapers to yourself en route—providing you're bound for a country with reliable mail service.

If you're going to err on one side or the other, it may be better to just pack more. After all, diapers don't weigh much, and though they consume a lot of suitcase room, you'll be able to use the space for other things on your return journey. And hey, you're traveling with small kids—the concept of packing light probably went out the window a long time ago.

KID STUFF TO BRING

FOR KIDS IN DIAPERS

- ❑ Diapers
- ❑ Baby wipes
- ❑ Diaper-rash cream
- ❑ Baby powder
- ❑ Changing pad
- ❑ Toilet seat adapter or potty seat
- ❑ Two outfits and pajamas per day, outerwear, socks and undershirts
- ❑ Swimsuit, swim diapers, diaper cover

FOR BOTTLE-FED KIDS

- ❑ Baby formula
- ❑ Can opener, if needed
- ❑ Bottles or holders and liners
- ❑ Bottle nipples
- ❑ Rings
- ❑ Bottle caps
- ❑ Bottle brush
- ❑ Breast pump

FOR MOBILITY

- ❑ Car seat
- ❑ Baby carrier
- ❑ Collapsible stroller

BEDTIME

- ❑ Blankets
- ❑ Sleepwear
- ❑ Pacifiers and spares
- ❑ Your child's lovey
- ❑ Nightlight
- ❑ Portable crib

DIVERSIONS

- ❑ Road atlas
- ❑ Sand toys
- ❑ Toy tote

FEEDING TIME

- ❑ Snacks
- ❑ Familiar foods
- ❑ Baby cereal
- ❑ Bibs

- ❑ Drinks
- ❑ Paper towels
- ❑ Baby wipes
- ❑ Terrycloth towel
- ❑ Collapsible hook-on high chair

FOR OLDER KIDS

- ❑ One outfit per day
- ❑ Two extra tops
- ❑ An extra pair of pants
- ❑ Hair accessories
- ❑ Two swimsuits per child
- ❑ Swim goggles
- ❑ One nice outfit for dress
- ❑ An out-of-season outfit
- ❑ Sweatshirt, sweater
- ❑ Windbreaker, outerwear

- ❑ Shoes, extra laces
- ❑ Socks
- ❑ Undies

JUST IN CASE

- ❑ Medications your child may need
- ❑ Acetaminophen
- ❑ Thermometer
- ❑ Your pediatrician's phone and fax number and e-mail address

OTHER STUFF

- ❑ Babyproofing supplies
- ❑ Laundry kit
- ❑ Moist towelettes
- ❑ Paper towels
- ❑ Resealable plastic bags
- ❑ Toiletries

FLYING WITH A BABY OR TODDLER?

Do be sure to pack lots more diapers, food, formula, and juice in your carry-on than you expect to need. What with delays, cancellations, and reroutings, a two- or three-hour trip can easily triple or quadruple in length (or worse). Worrying about running out of essentials is one hassle you won't need.

FOOD AND DRINK If the water supply at your destination is iffy, bring canned baby formula at least to get you started. Otherwise, transfer your formula powder to a resealable plastic bag to save weight and space.

If you're flying, you can't count on meal service at the hours your children will want to be fed. Check to see what will be served, and pack accordingly—or risk tantrums (yours, at the flight attendants). Stick with cubes of cheese, pasta, cut-up vegetables and fruit, the ubiquitous Cheerios, and other no-sugar snacks, and store them in resealable sandwich bags or small plastic tubs with snap-on lids; refillable sports bottles make a good alternative to juice boxes.

THE CAR SEAT QUESTION You may want to bring your child's car seat. Rental car companies can provide one but only by advance arrangement, and you may not like what you get. On airplanes, as in cars, babies and toddlers are safer in a car seat. Unfortunately, this can be an expensive proposition: children under two fly free if they sit on your lap (and are often permitted to ride in their car seats at no extra cost when space is available), but parents who haven't bought their youngsters a ticket must hold their offspring on their lap on a flight that's full.

THE TOY TOTE A portable stash full of toys, books, and activities can be a godsend. Holly, a travel writer who has three young children, keeps on hand a large tote devoted to travel toys—one-piece items that a sitting child can fiddle with happily for several minutes at a time. ("One-piece" is the operative term—ever try to pick up 50 tiny Lego bricks from underneath an airplane seat?) Her tote includes everything from handheld electronic games and Silly Putty to those cheap little puzzles with sliding tiles in a plastic tray, a Magic Slate (lift the gray film layer and your picture goes bye-bye), and a Woolly Willy (use a magnet to put metal-shaving hair and whiskers on bald Willy). Travel writer Eileen does the same thing, except she wraps hers individually and hands them out at the airport while the family is waiting for their turn to board.

This works: Holly recounts the story of a plane trip to Florida when her family sat behind a couple with a two-year-old boy who screamed and wailed for the first half hour of the flight. Finally, Holly reached over the seat and started handing him toys from her tote. The parents were astonished to find that their child remained quiet so long as he was entertained.

Karen swears by coloring/activity books and a small clipboard with note pad and pencils (good for tic-tac-toe, hangman, math practice, etc.). She packs one of these kits for each of her two daughters in a gallon-size resealable plastic bag. Crayons and washable markers go into these for trips on airplanes, colored pencils for car trips. "Don't take crayons in the car," she warns, "unless you don't mind having your seat-back pockets and compartments coated with thin, waxy crayon film." Though crayons don't puddle until the temperature climbs to 150°, they soften at a mere 100°—thus the mess.

Watch out for nonwashable markers anywhere. The odd uncapped marker is sure to slip unnoticed out of your child's hand, only to bleed profusely on your car's beige upholstery or—worse—on your spouse's expensive light wool trousers. Crayola's new line of Wonder markers, which show their true colors only when used on a specific kind of paper, were made for traveling.

Karen, Eileen, and Holly are always on the lookout for new items to add to their totes, and they never let their kids get into the bags between trips, lest they wear out their interest in those particular toys.

WHAT TO PUT IN YOUR TOY TOTE

- ❏ Action figures
- ❏ Balls
- ❏ Baseball mitt, gloves
- ❏ Batteries, adapter cables
- ❏ Books, books on tape
- ❏ Brain Quest games
- ❏ Bubble stuff
- ❏ Cards
- ❏ Checkers, chess (Velcro type)
- ❏ Clipboard
- ❏ Coloring/activity books
- ❏ Crayons, pencils, colored pencils, Wonder Markers
- ❏ Doll with outfits
- ❏ Etch-a-Sketch
- ❏ Finger puppets
- ❏ Game Boy, cartridges, light
- ❏ Jump ropes
- ❏ Lap desk
- ❏ Mad Libs
- ❏ Magic pen books
- ❏ Magic Slate
- ❏ Modeling clay
- ❏ Movies, movie player, batteries, adapter plug
- ❏ Music on CDs, tapes, or MP3 disks
- ❏ Note pad, drawing paper
- ❏ One-piece toys
- ❏ Play Doh
- ❏ Silly Putty
- ❏ Sliding puzzles
- ❏ Songbook
- ❏ Stickers
- ❏ Toy cars
- ❏ Travel toys
- ❏ Walkman
- ❏ Woolly Willy
- ❏ Word-search books

On car trips, take an inflatable beach ball, a soccer ball to kick around, or just a tennis ball. Or a baseball bat, ball, and mitts. Jump ropes also help kids burn off energy at rest stops.

THAT'S ENTERTAINMENT Vacation is a great time to take a break from TV, and your toy tote will take you far. But if it matters to you, check on whether you'll have a VCR or DVD player in your hotel room or can rent one. Even if there will be one, some families traveling by car in the States bring one along in the car; a small TV with a built-in VCR or DVD player, supplied with electricity via an adapter plug, can vastly reduce the number of are-we-there-yets you'll hear en route. In flight, a portable DVD player and a movie can also make time fly, but you have to bring your own electricity—pack extra batteries just in case.

No matter what your transportation, a book of travel games helps, too, and can start you having fun together before you get there.

CLOTHES AND USEFUL ITEMS Holly always packs a spare bath towel—useful for cleaning up spills and, until then, as a blanket. Her kids are active, so she always brings two swimsuits per child, so there's always a dry one to slip into. (And she brings them along on every trip—you never know.) If you're going to be in crowds, take bright clothes; your kids will stand out. However, dark clothes don't show dirt, so there are trade-offs. Even more important, take things your child really likes.

BAG 'EM

Organize toddlers' clothes into outfits—tops, bottoms, socks, and underwear—and put each outfit into its own resealable plastic bag. Put the child's name on the outside of the bag. Makes getting dressed in the AM a cinch.

In case of temperature changes, Wendy slips in one out-of-season outfit for each of her two sons, long pants in summer and shorts in spring and fall. A fleece jacket is cozy for the occasional chilly times on an otherwise warm-weather vacation. A laundry kit is a must; even if your trip is short, you'll want to pretreat stains to keep them from setting.

BRING THE LOVEY? Do you take the comfort object and risk losing it, or leave it behind? Opinions are divided. One Fodor's parent cut his daughter's blankie in half (after consultation). Half travels where she does; the other half stays home. If your child permits, add an iron-on label with your name, home address, and phone number.

ET CETERA, ET CETERA, ET CETERA Before your trip, start compiling a list of items that you use every day; sit down calmly and consider how important they will be on your trip; and bring along whatever you can't live without. You may want to prepare a special toiletries kit for your child: baby shampoo, bubble bath, lotion, and detangler or conditioner.

Consider whether you'll want to babyproof your hotel room or rental home; if so, acquire extra outlet covers and cabinet locks (or use duct tape).

Insect repellent, anti-itch remedies, and sunscreen are essential on almost every family trip. And if you'll be traveling abroad, make sure you have a plug adapter to use with your child's nightlight.

ONE-PARENT TRIPS ABROAD Remember, some countries require a parent traveling with kids to have a notarized letter from the absent parent granting permission to make the trip. Whenever you travel internationally, check immigration requirements well before you leave home.

ABOUT YOUR LUGGAGE Duffels are well suited for packing kids' clothes, since wrinkles are generally not an issue. If you've got small children, though, a travel pack may be a better bet, since it leaves a parent's hands free to push a stroller or hold a child's hand. When packing, include some garments belonging to each family member in every suitcase—this way, if one bag goes missing, you'll all still have something to wear. Give each walking child his or her own small backpack for en route snacks and toys. Don't, however, expect young children to handle their own carry-on suitcases; better to check one large bag and have fewer pieces of luggage to track.

▶ Resort Vacations

Here, the object is to get away and relax. But even Florida, Hawaii, the Caribbean, and Mexico have their own codes of dress and behavior.

GET SAVVY ABOUT SPORTS GEAR Know in advance what sports are offered at your resort, and for everything you plan to do, come with appropriate attire, including footwear— golf shoes, tennis shoes, aqua socks, whatever you'll need. Few resorts require tennis whites, but it's a good idea to bring them; white clothes are cooler in the sun anyway. If there's horseback riding on-site, pack a pair of jeans and shoes with heels.

Call the resort to find out what equipment you can rent on-site, then decide whether you want to bring your own.

If water sports are a mainstay, bring two bathing suits so you can wear one while the other's drying. You may want to bring your own beach towels.

SWIMSUIT PROTOCOLS You may spend the day in a bathing suit and T-shirt or cover-up, perhaps a sarong or pareo. But at least outside the United States, women should save short shorts and micro-minidresses for the pool or resort grounds. Walking shorts and polo shirts, T-shirts, or sundresses are better suited for shopping in town. For daytime sightseeing, men may wear T-shirts or polo shirts, shorts, and either sneakers and socks or boat shoes without socks.

WHAT'S UP WHEN THE SUN GOES DOWN? In the evening, depending on the formality of the resort or restaurant, men might want to switch to a long-sleeve shirt or polo shirt and long pants, either jeans or khakis. Jackets and ties are seldom required—call the resort in advance to be sure. Women can wear anything from a top and skirt to a chic cotton pants outfit or a pretty sundress, short or long.

REALITY CHECK

If you have a brochure from your resort, just glance at its photos. That's your best clue as to the resort's formality level.

HANDY BRING-ALONGS Don't forget a camera and a couple of rolls of film, tape for your video camera, or extra memory cards or memory sticks and batteries or battery charger, plug adapter, and converter for your digital camera. And consider throwing in a roomy tote bag as a convenient, if not totally secure, place to stash it poolside. Finally, don't forget sunscreen (it'll be cheaper at home) and, if you're at all sensitive to the sun, a sun hat.

PRECAUTIONS On resort trips, as in the city, it's best to avoid unnecessary displays of jewelry and cash.

ABOUT YOUR LUGGAGE What you'll pack for a resort destination depends on where you're headed and the level of formality you expect. At casual places you can roll all your clothing into a duffel bag. If you're staying at a more formal property, you may opt for a lightweight garment bag for fancier clothing and a wheeled suitcase for the rest.

▶ Theme Park Vacations

If you're bound for the Orlando-area theme parks, comfort is a prime concern—comfort in hot weather, most notably. Shorts and sneakers are the order of the day in summer, and that's obvious enough, but there are a few tricks.

Sunscreen sounds obvious, but you'd be surprised how many families emerge from their first day in the Magic Kingdom looking like the main course at the Red Lobster. Florida sun is simply stronger than most northerners expect it to be, and a little goes a long way. For this reason, a T-shirt is preferable to a bathing-suit top for women over shorts.

A sun hat also offers good sun protection, particularly the kind with a flap that covers the back of your neck.

WAYS TO CHILL OUT If there's anything that feels hotter than Phoenix in July, it may be Orlando (or any other theme park) when the weather's hot. Black-topped parking lots are huge open-air ovens, and concrete walkways in the park proper are not much better.

Fabrics such as Cool Max and Supplex, which wick perspiration away from your body and dry fast, keep you cooler. You'll find just how important that quick-drying feature is after you've gotten soaked through on one of the parks' water rides; with regular cotton shorts, you'll be soggy for hours.

Away from water rides, spritz yourself with a small sprayer that you can refill as needed; the "squeeze-and-breeze" version with a battery-operated fan attached is the ultimate in theme-park kitsch (they're way less expensive if you bring them from home, although you can buy them in the parks— and you'll be tempted for sure).

DON'T BE FOOTSORE Pay attention to your feet as well. Underneath your comfortable, well-broken-in sneakers, wear well-padded socks made from moisture-wicking, quick-drying fiber. Carry a spare pair of sneakers in your day pack or lightweight nylon tote bag (you may be able to leave these in lockers on the way into the park); change in midafternoon and your feet will reward you with a few more hours of faithful service. Add a bit of refreshing witch hazel or astringent for an ultracooling switch.

PLAN FOR COLD WEATHER In winter, the theme parks are still going strong and it's still hot, if not as hot as summer—but only by day. Things really cool down at night, and in early morning and in late afternoon, the wet rides can leave you cold; again the quick-drying feature comes in handy.

The best plan is to wear fleece jackets to the park in the morning, check them in the guest lockers when the day warms up, and reclaim them toward evening—you'll be glad you took the extra trouble.

THE LITTLE THINGS THAT MEAN SO MUCH Take an autograph book if you have kids (or prepare to buy one on the spot). Kids have fun with their own disposable cameras—more expensive inside theme parks, so buy them at home. And bring plenty of film, since it tends to be more expensive inside theme parks.

3

THE PLAN

Once upon a time there was a bright, creative man who was, alas, somewhat disorganized. For a week's business trip in the Caribbean—which he had been told in advance would involve island-hopping in tiny planes—he packed three large duffel bags, each one half empty. Because he was traveling to a warm-weather destination, his fellow travelers wondered what all those bags contained. But it all became frighteningly clear at the airport, as he unzipped a duffel so he could find his missing airplane ticket. Inside, he had a family-size box of tissues, magazines and books, swim trunks, a large beach towel, 10 or 12 compact disks, and a full-size shampoo bottle. A patina of baby powder covered everything—everything except the airplane ticket, which was nowhere to be found. Stuffed in among the balled-up shirts, shorts, and slacks in the next duffel were three pairs of shoes, a full-size iron, and a canister of tennis balls. Still no ticket. On to the third duffel, which contained cameras, film, recording equipment, miscellaneous papers—and the airplane ticket. By the time he began to search for his passport, the compulsive packers on the trip were dying to give him a packing lesson he'd never forget.

No matter how often we pack, certain dilemmas remain evergreen: How much to take without taking too much? How to fit it all in? How to remember crucial items? It's all about having a plan—and a wardrobe plan is only the beginning of it. Don't have a plan? Don't worry. With a little coaching, you, too, can formulate a packing strategy an Army general would envy.

TOP 10 STEPS TO NO-STRESS PACKING

- ❑ Start far ahead.
- ❑ Research baggage limitations.
- ❑ Make and keep travel kits.
- ❑ Work out your packing list.
- ❑ Think through your trip in detail.
- ❑ Stick with your plan.
- ❑ Master several folding techniques.
- ❑ Use plastic.
- ❑ Edit as you pack— take only what you can't live without.
- ❑ Save your list.

First Steps—Far Ahead

Packing is like most enterprises in life: the better the plan going in, the more successful the venture will be. (Witness: Desert Storm as opposed to Vietnam, *Star Wars* as opposed to *Water World*, etc.)

The most sensible approach is to complete various tasks over a period of time, so that much of the last-minute pressure is relieved. This assumes the optimistic view of the world, in which you'll have months of happy anticipation before your trip. In reality, you'll probably be told on Friday afternoon that you're expected Sunday morning for a week of meetings in Paris, and will spend the next 24 hours frantically throwing things into a valise. In one memorable Fodor's poll, 42.5% of the respondents confessed that they usually pack the day before or a few hours before they leave on a trip—and no doubt many of them had no one else to blame for this but their own procrastinating selves.

Still, there's a world of difference between hysterically flinging things into a suitcase and swiftly but thoughtfully assembling your gear. The idea is to start thinking about the process of packing as soon as you start thinking about taking a trip.

If you always have a series of travel kits packed and at the ready, you're one step ahead of the game. Then, your packing will already be under way when you finally buy the tickets or when you notify your office about when you'll be gone.

The first step is to begin to draw up a casual itinerary. Then research airline regulations and find out more about your destination. Investigate dress norms, and start thinking about your wardrobe. (For pointers, *see* Chapter 2.)

▶ Check with Your Airline

If your trip involves airlines, start by researching baggage regulations for every carrier and every flight segment on your itinerary, both on the way out and for your return trip. Find out the weight limits and the permissible number of carry-ons for each segment, remembering that regulations may well vary from flight to flight. You can often find out underseat dimensions and measurements of the stow bins overhead as well, either by phoning the carrier or checking its Web site. Then you can choose your luggage and plan your packing for the most restrictive segment.

BAGGAGE RULES OF THUMB In the United States, most airlines allow passengers to check two pieces of luggage and to carry on one additional bag, which must fit either into the overhead bin or underneath the seat in front of you, plus a personal item such as a briefcase, handbag, or diaper bag. Many carriers limit the dimensions of your primary carry-on to a total of no more than 45 inches—that is, 22 x 14 x 9, for example, or 20 x 16 x 9. The limit on your second carry-on is less a matter of size than of perception. It must look like a personal accessory such as a purse, briefcase, small knapsack, or diaper bag. The standard is subjective, however, so if you can fit one item into another—say, cram your handbag into your briefcase or your briefcase into a shopping bag—then go for it.

Each checked item must weigh no more than 70 pounds, and the height, width, and length of each must total no more than 62" or you may be charged a fee, which ranges from $50 to $150 per overlimit bag. Weight and size limits also apply to international flights that arrive in or depart from the United States.

COMMON EXCEPTIONS Between international destinations, weight limits are sometimes more restrictive. For instance, in many non-U.S. airlines, you are permitted to check no more than 44 pounds in coach, or 66 pounds if you're traveling in first class. For anything over that amount, you are asked to pay a surcharge—usually a charge per additional pound. (If you are carrying more than that, be prepared for a shock. It could cost you several hundred dollars.) If you are flying on a regional jet or other small plane, still other limits may apply. On small jets, you usually have to check small roller suitcases and garment bags at the gate and can bring only personal items on board. In other cases you may be weighed along with all your bags to make sure the plane isn't overloaded.

AVOID THESE CARRY-ON SNAFUS Both the underseat space and overhead bins vary in size from plane to plane. On some, the underseat space on the window side narrows a bit toward the floor because of the curve of the aircraft fuselage. On other planes, the space underneath the aisle seats is narrower because of the legs supporting the row of seats at the aisle end. In both situations, although you can usually stuff in something soft-sided, a stiff-sided carry-on simply may not fit. Similarly, some overhead bins are roomier than others.

Many airlines have installed templates at check-in counters and at departure gates, so you can find out whether your carry-ons will fit into the available space before attempting the same exercise on board. Still, it's a good idea to know the score beforehand, after you have researched the exact dimensions of the overheads and underseat spaces, take the time to measure your bag before you pack and again after you've filled it to make sure it conforms. Then you can go to Plan B if necessary before you head for the airport. Sometimes it's as easy as pulling things out of the bag's outside pocket and stuffing them into corners inside; sometimes the suitcase itself is the problem.

In other cases it's a question of timing. Sometimes all overheads are full by the time you board—perhaps an entire college marching band has just boarded the flight and filled every bin with their high-plumed red hats (true story!). Or it's the holidays and everyone and his sister has boarded bearing shopping bags full of presents.

In situations like these, if you're among the last to board and your carry-on doesn't fit under the seat that you were assigned, you will be asked to check your bag. Remember *Meet the Parents?* The whole plot kicks into gear when Greg, the Ben Stiller character, is forced to check his suitcase at the gate—and when he does so, neglects to remove the diamond engagement ring he intends to present to Pam, his nursery school teacher-girlfriend. The airline loses the bag, and things go downhill from there.

Anticipate problems with jumbo shopping bags containing corrugated cardboard boxes. If the boxes inside are too big, there is no way the bag will go under the seat, and when you force it, the bag will tear. Unless you know for a fact that there will be plenty of room in the overheads—and that the overheads are big enough—you're better off to bite the bullet and ship the thing.

DON'T COUNT ON THE CLOSET Do remember that larger items, including garment bags, infant car seats, and strollers, may have to be stowed in the small closet at the front of the cabin—but since this space fills up fast, you can't be sure you will be able to use it. Some one-class, single-aisle planes often used on domestic flights don't even have a closet. Items such as a stroller, which you need until the moment you board the plane, can usually be checked right at the gate.

RESEARCH SPECIAL CASES If you're going to be carrying a violin, guitar, or other special object, ask your airline in advance whether you will be required to check it. It's a good idea to note the name of the person you spoke with and record the date of your conversation.

If your contact can direct you to the specific section of the airline's conditions of carriage (the legal document that spells out what the airline will and will not do in all kinds of situations, usually posted on the Web), print out the appropriate section and have it in hand in case you have a problem.

FIND OUT ABOUT FOOD While you're talking to your airline, find out whether food will be served in flight. Ask about special meals if the answer is yes—sometimes these are a bit tastier than what's served to the hoi polloi—or plan to bring your own if there will be none.

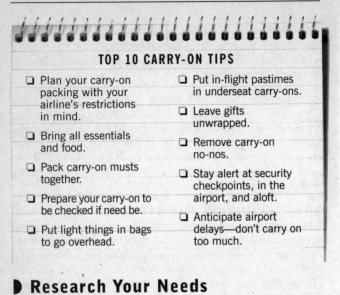

TOP 10 CARRY-ON TIPS

❑ Plan your carry-on packing with your airline's restrictions in mind.

❑ Bring all essentials and food.

❑ Pack carry-on musts together.

❑ Prepare your carry-on to be checked if need be.

❑ Put light things in bags to go overhead.

❑ Put in-flight pastimes in underseat carry-ons.

❑ Leave gifts unwrapped.

❑ Remove carry-on no-nos.

❑ Stay alert at security checkpoints, in the airport, and aloft.

❑ Anticipate airport delays—don't carry on too much.

▶ Research Your Needs

As you research any luggage restrictions you'll encounter, start thinking about what suitcase you will take. At the same time, start considering your wardrobe. But don't forget about other things you'll need. Think carefully about each item. Hundreds of things *could* come in handy along the way. Do you really need to take them all? Some you can pick up as you travel at no greater cost than at home. Some are too heavy or too bulky to warrant taking, given your available packing space or weight limitations. Remember, you're almost always better off traveling light—you can never count on skycaps or baggage carts being there when you need them.

If you pack with the expectation that you will always have to deal with your own bags, you won't be sorry. Too often, that's the way it will be.

STUDY THE DESTINATION Find out whether the things you use regularly—toiletries and personal hygiene items, film, baby supplies, and such—will be available at your destination. Fodor's gold guides usually include this information, or you can ask your travel agent, tour operator, or friends who have just traveled there. Look into clothing norms and customs as well. If you'll be visiting friends and family or *their* friends and family, think about the appropriate hostess gifts. (Possibilities include balloons or stickers for kids, a picture book or calendar from your hometown, a local cookbook, sports logo items, or the like. Pack wrapping paper, a small coil of ribbon, and a bit of tape to wrap these; if you carry gifts with you on a plane, you need to leave them unwrapped for clearing security.)

CALL YOUR HOTELS Inquire about in-room hair dryers, irons, ironing boards, cribs, high chairs, complimentary toiletries, and other amenities. Knowing you can leave some or all of these items at home will help you pare down your packing list and lighten your suitcase.

Also find out whether laundry facilities are on the premises or whether laundry service is available (and, if it is, what the turnaround time is); being able to have laundry done means you can pack less.

AN ELECTRIFYING TRIP? Based on the information you get from your hotels, think about electrical equipment you might want to take and, if you're headed abroad, look into the plug styles and current in your destination.

PLAN FOR WATER If you're bound for a developing nation, research water potability and, if necessary, think about whether you want to take a portable water purification system.

GET PAPERWORK IN ORDER Check to see that you (and your traveling companions) have valid passports—that is, passports that will still be valid the month after you expect to return. Also make sure you have obtained any necessary visas.

To apply for or renew a passport by mail, it's important to leave yourself some time: about four to five weeks for a new one, three to four weeks to renew one. If it's an emergency situation and you simply don't have that much time, you can apply in person at a U.S. Passport Office, which will try to

expedite your request for an additional fee. To all you pro-
crastinators out there: take care of your passport in advance.
Doing it in person is painfully time consuming, although various businesses—check the Yellow Pages or the Web—will
happily arrange for someone to do any necessary in-person
waiting for you for a fee. They can get you a passport
quickly—often within a day if your circumstances require it.

NEED SHOTS? Check a guidebook or call the Centers for
Disease Control to get information about any inoculations required in your destination.

CALL YOUR INSURANCE COMPANY Check to make
sure that your home-owner's or renter's insurance policy covers
losses away from home and that your health coverage will take
care of any medical needs that may arise, given your destination. If it doesn't, you may want to purchase a special travel
insurance policy or a baggage insurance policy just for the trip.

▶ Get Busy—Go Shopping

Now that you've laid the groundwork, it's time to start im-
plementing your plans. If you don't have travel kits already
compiled and at the ready, hop to it (*see below*). Pay special
attention to your personal documents kit, which involves
quite a bit of legwork.

Start shopping for useful and essential items—make the
rounds of your local merchants and study mail-order catalogs
and travel-specialist Web sites to acquire any travel aids you
think might be useful. If your luggage is shot, read Chapter 1
and start looking around.

BUY GUIDEBOOKS AND MAPS They'll help you
make decisions about what to take and help you finesse your
itinerary.

WORK ON YOUR WARDROBE Does your wardrobe
plan require a comfortable pair of oxford-style shoes that will
take you to the city sights by day and the theater at night? A
dressy blouse that will turn your suit skirt into a dinner outfit?

A special wrinkleproof black travel outfit or nifty multipocketed vest from a mail-order catalog? Get them now.

Go through your own clothes and decide what will need to be washed, dry-cleaned, and hemmed—and get it done.

Do a test wash on new clothing you plan to launder en route, to make sure it comes out well and dries easily.

TRY ON CLOTHES

If you're traveling with children, ask your youngsters to put on their vacation clothing in advance. If they have outgrown key items, don't wait until the night before the trip to replace them.

HANDLE MONEY MATTERS Now's the time to request a second ATM card as backup, in case yours is demagnetized. While you're at it, if you're traveling abroad, where ATMs usually take PIN numbers with only four digits, go to the bank and get a four-digit PIN number. Also, if your PIN number is alphabetical, make sure that you figure out its numerical translation, because on some keypads abroad, numbers are all you'll find.

TAKE CARE OF YOUR HEALTH Make an appointment with your doctor to get the shots you need. Do this early: some shots must be administered over a period of weeks, and others take time to become active. If you're traveling to countries where health advisories apply, speak with your doctor about malaria pills or other preventive medicine.

If you plan to be on the road for more than a couple of weeks, visit the dentist if you're due.

HIT THE DRUGSTORE While you're at it, make sure you have enough of any prescription medication and/or vitamins you need to take—count out enough doses to last you for the length of your trip plus a few days beyond, in case you are unavoidably detained. Replace any medications that have expired as well as any old sunscreen. If seasickness is a problem or you think it may be, look into seasickness remedies such as Dramamine or Sea Bands, which work by acupressure.

TO PACK OR NOT TO PACK: ELECTRICALS

Hair dryers and travel irons are a major cause of night-before agonizing—to pack or not to pack? If your hairstyle truly requires a blow-dry to look decent or if you really need to wear that easily wrinkled shirt, call ahead to your hotel to see if dryers and irons are available—most upscale hotels these days have them. If you travel often, it may be worth your while to invest in lightweight travel models. However, although both can come in handy when you need to make your freshly hand-laundered clothing dry faster, they do add bulk you don't need. And they're heavy and require a voltage converter and plug adapter abroad, which are also heavy. Many a traveler blows out the motor in a perfectly good hair dryer by forgetting to bring both.

What?

Yes, if you're going out of the country, you'll probably need both items—the converter to adapt the standard voltage at your destination into something your appliance can use, and the adapter to adapt the two-vertical-prong plug on the end of the electrical cord to fit local outlets.

Many foreign countries use a standard 220-volt current, which is different from the United States' 110 volts. The general rule of thumb is that the Eastern Hemisphere uses 220 volts, and Western Hemisphere countries use 110 volts, but there are plenty of exceptions—notably Argentina, Antigua, Chile, Guadeloupe, Honduras, Paraguay, St. Kitts/Nevis, St. Lucia, St. Vincent, and Uruguay, all of which use 220 volts even though they're in the Western Hemisphere.

BE ENTERTAINED Think about how you'll pass transportation time. Ask friends to recommend books for your trip—good beach reading, a novel set in your destination, or a great piece of travel literature. Books in English are often

As for plugs, there are five standard pin configurations:

- A, with flat parallel blades, like we use in the United States

- B, with two round pins, used in England and Germany

- C, with three rectangular prongs, used in England and Hong Kong

- D, with two round pins in a skinnier plug, à la France

- E, with flat angled blades, found in Australia and New Zealand

There is absolutely no rule of thumb to use here, except that A plugs are most common in the 110-volt countries. You'll be perfectly fine with your U.S. appliances in Canada, Mexico, Japan, Korea, Jamaica, Bermuda, and the Bahamas, as well as in U.S. territories such as Guam, Puerto Rico, and the U.S. Virgin Islands. Beyond that, you have to look up the electrical specifics of your destination in a travel guide before you go.

It's also essential to buy the adapters before you go—they won't be available in the country you're going to (there, stores sell adapters that change B pins to A pins, not the other way around).

Confused? Think long and hard about whether you really need to take your appliances at all. If you need a computer for work, that's one thing, but if you can eliminate the hair dryer, the shaver, and the travel iron, you'll avoid the whole issue.

hard to find or expensive outside English-speaking countries. (Don't overdo it, though. If you're planning to be gone for a long time, you can often borrow something from a fellow traveler.)

Earplugs can help you block out your neighbors' in-flight conversations, and a sleep mask and neck pillow, perhaps inflatable, can help you grab some shut-eye at odd times. A book light can enable you to read in trains and doubles as a flashlight. Simple playing cards can yield many hours of diversion; learn a few card tricks before you go and you can make some new friends as well. A CD player, a portable DVD player, or a cassette player and some books on tape can make time pass more quickly during layovers and long drives. A shortwave radio can help you stay in touch with the outside world when you're far away from home. (Or maybe you'd rather forget about all that!)

SHOP FOR LUGGAGE ACCESSORIES While you're in the luggage store or looking around on luggage-specialist Web sites, think about how you'll pack your suitcase. You may want to consider buying packing envelopes, which help you sort and segregate different kinds of objects inside your suitcase. If you need them, pick out luggage tags, a luggage strap, and locks for your suitcase. Consider a luggage alarm if you think you might occasionally be forced to leave your luggage untended for periods of time.

STAY IN TOUCH Walkie-talkies can be fun on some kinds of trips—when you're on the ski slopes or anywhere else where your group wants to split up and stay in touch but cell phones aren't an option. For settled areas within the United States—say, when your group wants to split up to wander around an airport during a delay—a pair of cell phones works instead. Make sure your equipment and your service will work at your destination and make adjustments as needed.

PLAN FOR ELECTRICAL ACCESSORIES For any electrical equipment you want to bring, get an electrical current converter and plug adapter if you don't already have one. A battery eliminator can be useful and comes in dual-voltage versions. Extra batteries for anything you're taking that's battery-operated are a must if you'll be traveling in developing nations—but think about leaving these items at home. Consider the weight and ask yourself if they're really essential.

OF PICNICS AND POTABLES A water bottle is good for most kinds of trips. (If you're traveling into areas without potable water, bring a water purification system or be prepared to boil, buy bottled stuff, or do without.)

And what about picnic supplies? Do you want to take a cooler for picnics on your driving trip? Plastic eating utensils are a must-pack. A collapsible cup is helpful for picnics and when you're not staying in hotels and motels where you can count on finding clean glasses.

An immersion heater and a mug can enable you to prepare dried cocoa, dried soups, or a cup of tea or coffee in your room; if you don't like instant coffee, you can bring your own drip cone, filter, and ground beans. Although this is really carrying things a bit far—the mug is heavy and the cone bulky—you may not mind if the cousins you're visiting serve only instant brew or if you're bound for a country such as Japan, where a good cup of coffee can do some real damage to your budget.

A super-absorbent towel such as those marketed to swimmers, campers, and tennis players (Packtowl® is one brand that comes in a variety of sizes) can be useful to wipe up spills, dry your hands, or any number of other things. Though compact, these nifty towels can soak up nine times their weight in liquid—and they dry fast.

IT'S A WASH Purchase laundry products if you want to take them. A bunch of resealable plastic bags in various sizes—snack size, sandwich size, quart size, and one- and two-gallon size—is essential. (These will isolate such objects as wet bathing suits and muddy shoes that are taking a long time to dry, or hold together collections of small objects you may gather in your travels—seashells, business cards, etc., which you can sort into the smaller bags. But they have many other uses. More about those later.)

COMPACT COMFORTS If you're traveling on the cheap, you may enjoy having a silk sleep sack—like a sleeping bag made out of silk but without a zipper—which you can snuggle into in less-than-pristine quarters. Silk compresses to almost nothing and dries fast when you wash it.

Also essential: small packs of tissues, which can be used for toilet paper in a pinch.

THINK SAFETY For some hotel rooms, a rubber doorstop may give you a sense of security. For walking around, you may want to acquire a security wallet or a money belt that you can use to safely and comfortably carry your cash, traveler's checks, passport, and essential credit cards. If you're heading into hot weather, make sure that the portion next to your body is of either mesh or a fabric that will wick away moisture. Women may want to think about a handbag with a steel cable in the strap (available from retailers and e-tailers who sell travel goods), if the trip will take you to locales where thievery is a problem.

Buy timers to put on your lamps at home.

MAKE MEMORIES LAST How about bringing a travel journal? Write your thoughts every day and use the glue stick in your portable office to paste in ephemera—tickets, brochures, pressed flowers, discarded luggage tags, boarding passes, matchbook covers, business cards, and such. A hardcover book will last longest; glue an envelope or two in the back to hold small items that you don't want to paste down.

Sometimes an audiocassette recorder can be fun, as a souvenir of the sounds of your trip.

PLAN FOR SNAPSHOTS Photos are forever. Do bring enough film to last your entire trip (and then some—more is particularly important if you're traveling outside the United States or staying in resort areas, where prices tend to be high). If your destination has reliable postal services, you may want to buy prepaid photo mailers. You can pop an exposed roll of film into one of these and have the prints mailed back to your home; they'll be waiting for you, already developed, upon your return.

If you plan to use a digital camera, make sure you have your battery charger (with a plug adapter and currency converter if necessary) or extra batteries. In addition, bring either extra memory sticks or memory cards; or pack your laptop and the camera cable so that you can download your images and free up your camera memory.

SHOP SMART If you plan to shop for something special at your destination, price the same kind of item around your hometown or on the Internet, so that you'll be able to recognize a good price when you see one. No point in carting something halfway around the globe if you can find the same thing at home for less.

If you think you might want to shop for your home, collect measurements—areas you might want to tile, windows you might find curtain fabric for, areas of wall where you might want to hang a picture, and so on. Gather paint chips and swatches so that you can match up possible acquisitions with things you already have—takes away the guesswork. Collect size information for people you want to buy presents for. Make notes on index cards and pack the cards in your personal documents kit.

TRAVEL AIDS YOU MAY WANT TO PACK

- ❏ Adapters, converter
- ❏ Alarm clock
- ❏ Audiocassette recorder
- ❏ Audiotapes, CDs
- ❏ Batteries
- ❏ Battery chargers
- ❏ Battery eliminator
- ❏ Binoculars
- ❏ Books on tape
- ❏ Book light
- ❏ Bungee cords
- ❏ Camera, lenses
- ❏ Camp towel
- ❏ Cassette/CD player
- ❏ Citronella candle
- ❏ Coffee-can lid
- ❏ Collapsible cup
- ❏ Compass
- ❏ Soft cooler
- ❏ Earplugs
- ❏ Flashlight
- ❏ Guidebooks
- ❏ Immersion heater, mug
- ❏ Inflatable hangers
- ❏ Luggage tags
- ❏ Luggage locks
- ❏ Luggage strap
- ❏ Luggage alarm
- ❏ Maps
- ❏ Money belt
- ❏ Money converter
- ❏ Neck pillow, possibly inflatable
- ❏ Photo film, digital-camera memory card
- ❏ Phrasebook
- ❏ Pillow
- ❏ Plastic eating utensils
- ❏ Playing cards
- ❏ Portable TV or DVD player
- ❏ Radio
- ❏ Rubber doorstop
- ❏ Sea Bands
- ❏ Silk sleep sack
- ❏ Sleep mask
- ❏ Tissues in small packs
- ❏ Travel iron
- ❏ Travel journal
- ❏ Video recorder, blank tapes
- ❏ Walkie-talkies
- ❏ Water bottle
- ❏ Water purification system

▶ The Next Steps

TAKE CARE OF BUSINESS Don't wait until the day before you leave to ask a kind neighbor or friend to keep an eye on things and be your contact at home while you're gone—start now. While you're at it, consider lining up a backup just in case. Be sure to equip him or her with your burglar alarm company's number and your code, and provide duplicates of important papers such as your itinerary, copies of your tickets and the first page of your passport, and the like.

Arrange to have your yard tended, your plants watered, your trash cans and recycling containers taken in, and your newspapers, mail, and deliveries collected while you are gone. (Some people insist that it's preferable not to stop delivery altogether, lest it become apparent that you're not in residence.) Call the kennel to arrange for pet care. Schedule a haircut. Change the batteries in your camera and your watch. If you really want to be compulsive, change your shoelaces, so that you don't end up with a broken one halfway through France.

HELP THE AIRLINES HELP YOU

Florida's Patricia Fairchild won an award in Wyndham Hotels' search for the savviest women business travelers for this tip: she always packs a photo of her suitcase in her briefcase, just in case the airline loses it.

I.D. ALL YOUR STUFF Label your luggage both inside and out—both luggage you plan to check and your carry-ons—with your name and contact information or your business card. If a thief gets a look at your home address, he's sure to head off on a little business trip of his own. Some airlines require that your tags bear an address—that's fine, just use your company's. If you work out of your home, be sure to include your firm's name to make it look more like a business address.

Make it as easy as possible for airlines to track you down—keep a copy of your itinerary, with your e-mail address and the phone number of a contact at home, inside your suitcase. If possible, stow this information in an unlocked outside pocket.

Also identify other possessions that are apt to get lost. Put a sticker with your name, address, phone number, and e-mail address on your umbrella, your electronic organizer, your cell phone, and your calculator. Pin a card with the same information in your jackets, sweaters, coats, and hats as well. You're more likely to get them back if people know where to send them.

PACKING FOR TWO?

If you are traveling with a companion, get your dual acts together: one of you packs the iron, the other takes the hair dryer, and so forth. Similarly, pack one complete outfit in your companion's suitcase, so you'll have something to wear in case your luggage goes missing; by all means return the favor. Take two credit cards. And each of you should carry half of the other's traveler's checks, just in case.

The chances are good that other people own the exact same luggage you do—it's inevitable. What's not inevitable is their taking your bag home by accident. Mark all your luggage (checked and carry-on, including your black laptop case that looks exactly like everybody else's black laptop case) with something that gives it personality and transforms it from an old bag into an experienced valise. Even carry-on aficionados who don't know the business end of a baggage carousel will appreciate this tip, as it works just as well in a crowded hotel lobby, in front of a motor coach, at a security checkpoint—wherever there's lots of luggage. Although monograms are helpful, they might be too subtle for a tired passenger who's just come off the red-eye from L.A. You might mark the side with your initials or a large X in duct tape. Or loop a bright orange bandanna around your suitcase handle. Or use a ribbon or neon green plastic streamer, a bungee cord or a luggage strap with your name on it, a garter belt, sausage links. Be creative, but also be careful: displaying an "Undertakers do it in the deep-freeze" sticker might result in a rather solitary vacation.

Make Your Travel Kits

Preparing an assortment of travel kits filled with important travel items will save you packing time and aggravation in the long run. Because the kits will have been prepared far in advance, you'll be less likely to forget something. Like Chris and Nina, who travel extensively for their jobs, just go ahead and buy two of everything—makeup, toiletries, etc.—and keep one set permanently packed inside your luggage.

With ingenuity, many items in your kits come in handy for uses beyond those you intended. Any kind of tape, for instance, can be used to remove lint. Dental floss can stand in for a broken shoelace in a pinch or be used to tie your zippers closed to deter thieves, in the event you forgot to bring locks. (Alternatively, you can use garbage-bag twist-ties or the little plastic thingies used to hold electrical cords together, available in stores such as Radio Shack.) Paper clips, paper clamps, and safety pins can be used to hold together drapes that don't quite close, so that you can get a little extra shut-eye the morning after a night on the town. And that's only the beginning.

▶ A Toiletries Kit

From the Mickey Mouse–themed bottles and jars stocked at Walt Disney World properties to the lavish Lanvin toiletries found at chic Paris hotels, it seems that almost every kind of accommodation today has amenities in the bathroom—shampoo and conditioner, a sewing kit, a shoe polisher, body lotion, etc. Even economy hotels have joined in, placing small baskets filled with washcloths, tiny bars of soap, and plastic flowers by their stall showers. Handy as they may be, however, the kits tend to lack certain essentials—toothpaste among them. Travelers loyal to a particular brand will undoubtedly want to bring their own stuff, no matter how elegant the freebies. So even if you call ahead to your hotel and verify that your bathroom contains an amenities basket, you'll still want to bring along some basic toiletries. The idea here is to select the smallest size of everything, keep it all in one convenient place, and guard against leakage.

WANT TO PACK A PUMP?

For toiletries stored in pump dispensers, tape a piece of cardboard between the pump and the lip of the bottle so that the pump cannot be depressed. (A dripping pump can be a real downer.)

These days, lots of personal-care products are available in small sizes—shaving cream, shampoo, conditioner, mouthwash, deodorant. Even name-brand cosmetics lines offer travel-size face creams and cleansers, often included in department store giveaways. (One Fodor's editor was notorious for refusing to go anywhere without his 12 different travel-size bottles of Kiehl's skin products—he even took them to the office.) Travel-size products save important packing space for crucial items available in full size only, such as the one styling gel in the world that works on your hair.

Buy travel-size products whenever you see them, so that you can replenish your stock as needed. Or buy small plastic bottles and the tiniest plastic jars, then refill as needed from your full-size housebound bottles. (The Container Store is a good resource for these—but there are many others.) Remember to fill jars and bottles only about five-sixths of the way up—changes in air pressure during a flight can cause the contents to expand and leak out of the top.

In hot weather, astringent can make your face feel cool or provide an instant pick-me-up to your feet.

Another thing that sometimes comes in handy: an extra pair of glasses. Bring your spare pair.

WHAT'S IN YOUR TOILETRIES KIT

- ❏ Astringent
- ❏ Bath soap
- ❏ Bottle opener*
- ❏ Cologne or perfume
- ❏ Comb and brush
- ❏ Spare contact lenses
- ❏ Contact-lens supplies
- ❏ Corkscrew*
- ❏ Cotton swabs
- ❏ Dental floss
- ❏ Deodorant
- ❏ Emery board
- ❏ Extra eyeglasses
- ❏ Eyedrops
- ❏ Eyeglass repair kit*
- ❏ Facial cleanser
- ❏ Feminine hygiene products
- ❏ First-aid kit *(see below)*
- ❏ Foot powder
- ❏ Hair conditioner
- ❏ Hair dryer
- ❏ Hair ties and clips
- ❏ Hand lotion
- ❏ Hand sanitizer
- ❏ Insect repellent
- ❏ Lip balm
- ❏ Magnifying mirror
- ❏ Makeup
- ❏ Matches
- ❏ Moisturizer
- ❏ Mouthwash
- ❏ Nail clippers
- ❏ Nail polish (clear)
- ❏ Nail polish remover
- ❏ Razor
- ❏ Sewing kit
- ❏ Shampoo
- ❏ Shaving cream
- ❏ Shoelaces
- ❏ Soap
- ❏ Styling gel, hair spray
- ❏ Sunscreen
- ❏ Swiss Army knife*
- ❏ Tissues
- ❏ Toilet paper
- ❏ Toothbrush
- ❏ Toothpaste
- ❏ Tweezers
- ❏ Washcloth
- ❏ Wipes

May be confiscated at airport security checkpoints. Take these out of your carry-on luggage.

THINK SHORTCUTS

Look for ways to make your daily habits more travel-friendly. After all, you are not going away forever. Women may wish to pack one all-purpose cream rather than individual hand, body, and face creams. Scented body cream is a good substitute for perfume. Cotton pads premoistened with nail polish remover are more practical, and safer to pack, than a bottle of the stuff. Some travelers, eager to travel light, gladly leave at home their contact lenses (and six different solutions and electric sterilizers), opting instead for the ease and simplicity of eyeglasses. Or, having planned in advance, they acquire disposable lenses. Men who travel light shave with a disposable razor rather than dealing with the hassles—and weight—of their usual electric shaver plus a current converter. Use an electric toothbrush? Leave it at home and buy a person-powered model—again, you're saving space, weight, and converter hassles.

Consider how to make each item easier or lighter to pack. Remove facial tissues from their bulky boxes, and slip the cardboard roll out of toilet paper; to keep these paper goods fresh, slip them into resealable sandwich bags. Ditto for baby wipes—good for no-water hand washing (and stain removal, according to some travelers).

Women should pack a day's supply of tampons or pads when traveling in the United States, a month's supply when traveling off the beaten path. For western Europe, choose one option or the other, depending on how willing you are to experiment with local brands or pay a bit extra to find products you're used to.

ESSENTIAL TOOLS For a savvy traveler such as Pete, the most important part of his kit is his Swiss Army knife. In mere inches of space, it equips him with scissors, a toothpick, a nail file, a bottle opener, a screwdriver, and a small knife. (Pete swears by the real McCoy, as he believes that other pocket knives are made from flimsy material and break easily.) But every Swiss Army knife has different components. If yours omits scissors, a corkscrew, or a screwdriver, by all means pack them—although in your checked luggage, since these components are now carry-on luggage no-nos. If you plan to carry everything on, leave your good Swiss Army knife at home and plan on acquiring a replacement at your destination.

JUST IN CASE Keep sunscreen in your kit, even if you're not headed for especially sunny climes. The way the ozone layer works these days, even an afternoon's sightseeing cruise in Stockholm could result in a sunburned nose.

BUG JUICE Some people recommend buying insect repellent in the country you are traveling to, rather than in the United States, on the theory that each country knows best what works on its own native bugs. Not true, and possibly dangerous. The Food and Drug Administration was set up to protect U.S. citizens from the hazards of harmful medications, chemicals, and other substances; few other countries have an equivalent organization. Therefore, the repellent you buy overseas might contain ingredients outlawed for use in the United States—ingredients that you may prefer not to douse yourself with. Buy repellent at home, and plan to use it when needed, limiting your exposure to insects in other ways. Cover as much of your body as possible by wearing long-sleeve shirts (light-colored for coolness), long pants, and socks. In some areas, citronella can be helpful; it comes in candles, in sticky pads you can affix next to your bed, and as coiled plastic bracelets that you can wear on wrists and ankles. Don't use perfumes or other scented products that may only make you more attractive to bugs. And stay inside during the hours when mosquitoes are hungriest, namely dawn and dusk.

STORING YOUR STASH Store your toiletries in a special case—one that's lined with plastic, please. A bag that's bright, cherry red, say, would be impossible to miss at the bottom of a black duffel or among a pile of white hotel towels (or beige, if the decorator felt absolutely daring). A gallon-size resealable bag, preferably freezer weight, also works; the contents are immediately obvious to all who look in your suitcase, including both the security screener probing your carry-on and the would-be thief in search of valuables in your hotel room. Load every toiletry item you think you will need into your kit, so that you can simply bring the whole thing into the bathroom and leave it there—it will spare you that desperate, dripping exit from the shower because your shampoo is still in the suitcase.

Some people seem to enjoy getting perfume on their cotton balls, shoe polish on the swabs, and toothpaste all over everything. If you don't, here's another foolproof tip for maintaining product individuality: subdivide your collection into subkits, each in a snack-size, sandwich-size, or quart-size bag; resealable bags simply can't be beat for holding small products, and they stop leaks from spreading through your entire kit. If you really like to be organized, you can make "product pals" out of your toiletries—put your travel-size shampoo and conditioner into one sandwich bag, your disposable razor and travel-size shaving cream in another, etc. Or all your shower stuff in one bag, and all the stuff you use next to the sink at another. (Sorting this all out is even more fun at 3 AM when you have to leave for the airport at 5 AM and you haven't even begun ironing yet.) After all this preparation, if you still wind up with Brylcreem on your Bruno Maglis, something larger than all of us is at work.

FRESH SUNSCREEN

The chemicals that give sunscreen its sun-protecting ability eventually lose their potency. Some products these days come imprinted with expiration dates; if you have a tube, check the crimp on the bottom; call the company's 800 number, on the package, if you need help deciphering the numbers. In any case, if the product is gritty or has separated, discard it. If you need fresh sunscreen for your trip, buy it before you go—the price is sure to be higher at your tourist-packed destination.

SEAT MATE It's a good idea to take at least your key toiletries kit on the plane, even when you have checked other luggage. The air in the cabin is pressurized and your carry-on will not be manhandled by baggage handlers— two reasons why messy leaks and spills are less likely. Also, you will have access to various items so that you can freshen up en route. (Have you ever tried to persuade a flight attendant to "dispense medication"—i.e., give you a Tylenol—for a headache?) And if your luggage is delayed or lost, or gets whisked into storage at a hotel where your room isn't ready, it's nice to have a toothbrush handy, especially after a long flight.

▌ The Laundry Kit

Even if you didn't plan to do laundry during your trip, it's helpful to travel with a few laundry supplies. When a stain shows up, you'll be glad to have a small bottle of detergent or Woolite (look for the travel-size packages—they're wonderful).

Club soda works on many stains, but a few other special supplies can be helpful as well. White vinegar dabbed on tomato-sauce spots will take them right out; put a towel or washcloth underneath the stain as you dab with a cotton ball or another piece of cloth. Carry some in a one-ounce bottle along with a couple of Shout gel wipes and dab the stain when it occurs. A special stain stick can also be helpful; for dry-cleanables, you need a spot remover.

An inflatable hanger or two takes no space. Ditto for a clothesline and clothespins (or get the braided kind of clothesline, which requires none).

To remove the inevitable wrinkles, a fabric relaxant such as Wrinkle Out usually does the trick, removing all but the most tightly set creases. Or you could take a mini–spray bottle (light in weight, but a bit bulky unless you empty out a sample-size hairspray bottle); spritz lightly with water, smooth the fabric with your hand, and hang to dry. Running a damp washcloth down the fabric instead of giving it a spritzing works in a pinch. Or you can try the old trick of steaming up your shower, then hang the garment overnight or until it dries.

Depending on where you're staying, you may be able to just call housekeeping for an iron and an ironing board, of course.

WHAT'S IN YOUR LAUNDRY KIT

- ❏ Clothesline
- ❏ Clothespins
- ❏ Fabric relaxant
- ❏ Hangers (inflatable)
- ❏ Laundry detergent
- ❏ Shout gel
- ❏ Sink stopper
- ❏ Spot remover
- ❏ Spray bottle
- ❏ Stain stick
- ❏ White vinegar

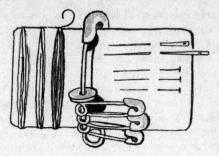

▶ The Sewing Kit

It's a funny thing about sewing kits. They seem fussy in a dowdy mother-hen kind of way. But a sewing kit lands firmly in the must-have category when the hidden button abruptly falls off your favorite wrap-around skirt—you know, the button that makes these garments look come-hither as opposed to come-and-get-it—and you find yourself having to rely on the folks in housekeeping to reattach the button, for a price you'd prefer not to think about. Moral of the story: sewing kits do come in handy and they can save you lots and lots of money. They also don't take up much room.

WHAT'S IN YOUR SEWING KIT

❑ Thread—light, medium, and dark

❑ Buttons

❑ Safety pins—large and small

❑ Needles

❑ Small blunt scissors

You can purchase a small sewing kit at your local five-and-dime or drugstore. Or make your own: String a handful of small safety pins and a few buttons (small white and black ones are fine) onto a larger safety pin. Pierce a credit-card-size piece of cardboard with a few straight pins and a couple of needles (one should have a large enough eye to take dental floss, which you can use for emergency repairs when strength is important). Wind a supply of white, black, and navy thread around the cardboard, pin the button-bearing safety pin across the thread as if it were a belt, and you're in business. For scissors, you need look no farther than your Swiss Army knife. If you don't have one of these or if you plan to carry everything on and must leave yours at home, blunt scissors will serve. (Remember that knives and pointed scissors are not permitted in carry-on luggage, so check them or leave them at home, lest yours be confiscated at a security checkpoint.) Place the card in a sandwich bag along with the scissors. Better yet, use one of those diminutive snack bags. Then pack the whole thing into your toiletries kit. You'll always have it with you, and you'll be a hit with travelers who have forgotten theirs.

▶ The First-Aid Kit

The well-traveled Pete possesses the nonpareil of first-aid kits. He keeps everything in an ancient metal Band-Aid box. Small yet serviceable, it has accompanied him everywhere from Bayonne, New Jersey, to Belize. His kit includes gauze pads, adhesive strips, dental floss, and premoistened antiseptic towelettes (for sterilizing and cleaning cuts and abrasions). He even used to carry a spare roll of film. There's enough of each of the medications in Pete's kit—cold pills, antidiarrheal pills, antacid, aspirin, acetaminophen—to last two days, as he figures that if he does fall ill on the road, he will be able to find more specific medical treatment in that time. You will probably need additional items if you plan to hike, camp, or otherwise travel in the forest, jungle, or other terrain away from civilization. And make sure you've got adequate birth control with you. Often, the moment you need it is long after the shops have closed, and even then, it's not always available.

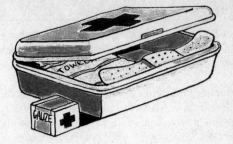

WHAT'S IN YOUR FIRST-AID KIT

❑ Adhesive strips
❑ Adhesive tape
❑ Analgesics
❑ Antacid
❑ Antibiotic cream
❑ Antidiarrheal pills
❑ Antiseptic towelettes
❑ Anti-itch stick for mosquito bites
❑ Birth control items

❑ Cold pills
❑ Cortisone cream
❑ Eyewash cup
❑ Eyedrops
❑ Gauze pads
❑ Medications you need
❑ Moleskin
❑ Nasal spray
❑ Thermometer (digital)

▶ The Personal Documents Kit

Maintain a pouch or envelope for miscellaneous travel documents, including any leftover traveler's checks from previous trips, copies of prescriptions for medications and eyeglasses, key medical information, a list of your frequent-flier and frequent-guest numbers, and your credit-card account numbers and their emergency refund telephone

JUST MARRIED?

If you were ticketed using your spouse's last name but your ID remains in your maiden name, bring your marriage license to back up your explanation.

numbers for your destination, as well as phone, fax, and cell phone numbers and snail-mail and e-mail addresses for all the key people in your life. (This would include family members, neighbors, your doctor, your lawyer, associates at work, and your travel agent; if he or she also has a 24-hour help line, include that as well.)

Add to this a copy of your insurance card, with your group and individual ID numbers and the company's phone and fax numbers. Include a photocopy of the first page of your passport. Some overseas-bound business travelers carry extra passport photos plus two official copies of their birth certificate. With these, another official passport can be issued in the event of loss or theft of the original, rather than just a temporary replacement.

Add your swatches and measurements cards—friends' sizes and measurements, hometown prices on things you want to buy, swatches of fabric of clothing or home furnishings you'd like to match, and paint chips.

Take a picture of your luggage and add that.

If you don't have all these documents on hand, get out your address book, stop by a photocopier, and put it all together now, whether or not you've got a trip in the offing. Even if you never get robbed or fall ill in a foreign country, being prepared is worth it for the peace of mind alone. Keep the envelope in your luggage. Give copies of all the important papers in your documents kit to a friend at home; you can also send the typed-up information in an e-mail to yourself that you can access on the road if need be.

Finally, make sure that your photo ID matches the name that's on your ticket or e-ticket confirmation.

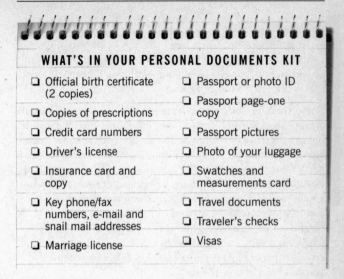

WHAT'S IN YOUR PERSONAL DOCUMENTS KIT

- ❑ Official birth certificate (2 copies)
- ❑ Copies of prescriptions
- ❑ Credit card numbers
- ❑ Driver's license
- ❑ Insurance card and copy
- ❑ Key phone/fax numbers, e-mail and snail mail addresses
- ❑ Marriage license

- ❑ Passport or photo ID
- ❑ Passport page-one copy
- ❑ Passport pictures
- ❑ Photo of your luggage
- ❑ Swatches and measurements card
- ❑ Travel documents
- ❑ Traveler's checks
- ❑ Visas

When it's time to travel, just add your airline tickets, hotel reservations documents or any other confirmations of prepaid travel information, maps of your destination, your guidebook, and more traveler's checks. Make a couple of copies of your travel documents as well. Put one copy separate from your personal documents kit, and leave one copy with your friend at home.

❚ The Portable Office

Having a small kit of often-used business items can be a real convenience on the road.

Bring letter-size envelopes to hold receipts as well as for correspondence, and 5" x 7", 8" x 10", 9" x 12", and 10" x 13" manila envelopes, which come in handy for sending brochures and papers home, so that you don't have to pack them in your luggage. Use a slightly bigger envelope or a large resealable plastic freezer bag as a pouch for all of the other materials. Sort small items into resealable plastic bags.

If you want to stay in touch on the road, connectivity equipment is important. You'll need the proper phone plugs and cables for your laptop, and perhaps a surge protector and diskettes. For your electronic organizer, you'll need still other cables or perhaps just a charger.

Some travelers bring preaddressed mailing labels to use to send postcards and letters home. If a family member will be having a birthday while you're on the road, bring a card—also preaddressed. Having a couple of note cards lets you write thank-you notes as the occasion arises during your trip. Business cards are good for exchanging addresses, even when you're not on business. Pack a marking pen as well, and you can label new possessions and old ones as you think of it. A candle comes in handy when the lights go out. If you replenish items as you run out, the next time a business associate cries, "A paper clip! A paper clip! My MBA for a paper clip!" you can smugly save the day.

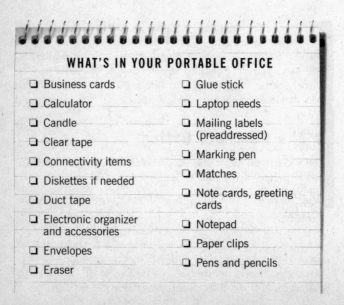

WHAT'S IN YOUR PORTABLE OFFICE

- ❏ Business cards
- ❏ Calculator
- ❏ Candle
- ❏ Clear tape
- ❏ Connectivity items
- ❏ Diskettes if needed
- ❏ Duct tape
- ❏ Electronic organizer and accessories
- ❏ Envelopes
- ❏ Eraser
- ❏ Glue stick
- ❏ Laptop needs
- ❏ Mailing labels (preaddressed)
- ❏ Marking pen
- ❏ Matches
- ❏ Note cards, greeting cards
- ❏ Notepad
- ❏ Paper clips
- ❏ Pens and pencils

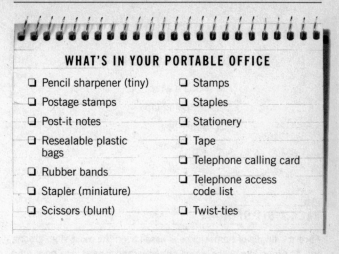

WHAT'S IN YOUR PORTABLE OFFICE

- ❑ Pencil sharpener (tiny)
- ❑ Postage stamps
- ❑ Post-it notes
- ❑ Resealable plastic bags
- ❑ Rubber bands
- ❑ Stapler (miniature)
- ❑ Scissors (blunt)
- ❑ Stamps
- ❑ Staples
- ❑ Stationery
- ❑ Tape
- ❑ Telephone calling card
- ❑ Telephone access code list
- ❑ Twist-ties

▌ For Passionate Shoppers

It may be a replica birch bark canoe, spied at an outfitters' store at the end of a week in Canada's Quetico wilderness. Or it may be three matching china vegetable dishes, complete with lids, which you find for a song at a Paris flea market. Or some other must-have. But you'd better face it from the get-go: even if you hate to shop, you'll probably find something you can't live without, sometime in your vacation.

If you intend to do some serious shopping, don't leave home without bubble wrap, scissors, strapping tape, and a good-size, totally collapsible tote bag. The former is useful for anything that's even vaguely breakable. Even when it might well be easy to find, who wants to waste valuable vacation time looking for a Staples? The latter will make it easy to consolidate your purchases and get them onto the plane. To see you through those days of shopping, when you don't want to carry your big tote from the beginning, a string bag can also come in handy and packs in almost no space.

SHOPPER'S SURVIVAL KIT

- ❏ Bubble wrap
- ❏ Strapping tape
- ❏ String bag
- ❏ Tape measure
- ❏ Tote bag

PACK A BIT OF HOME

Face it—tinges of homesickness assail even the most stoic among us. At times like these, familiar sights and flavors can go a long way. Some travelers like to pack a few food items that are hard to find on the road. This is mainly easy-to-pack stuff; Kathy, who hates Chinese food and routinely loads her suitcase with cans of tuna and jars of peanut butter for long business trips to Asia, is a notable exception. Herbal tea bags, on the other hand, are small and light, and can really provide a soothing lift when you need one most. If you can't tolerate caffeine, it might be wise to pack some single-cup portions of instant decaffeinated coffee to get you through those occasions when the only java available is the kind with a jolt. Remember your favorite sugar substitute, too—Equal comes in pill dispensers the size of Tic Tac boxes. Acting on the same principle, you may want to bring along something small to make your hotel room feel homier. A family picture (it needn't be framed) or a stuffed animal to sleep with at night instead of your significant other—these can do wonders to brighten up a sterile setting. You can use a favorite picture as a bookmark; it will also become a conversation piece. If you're going to be gone for a long time, photocopy a collage of favorite snapshots, and you can put them up, poster style, wherever you stay. Scented candles and bath salts are also nice to have on hand. And if this is a honey-moon, may your extras exceed your imagination!

Countdown to Packing

Isn't it exciting? You're almost on vacation . . . and you've taken care of everything suggested so far, right? If so, you're ready to move on to the next phase.

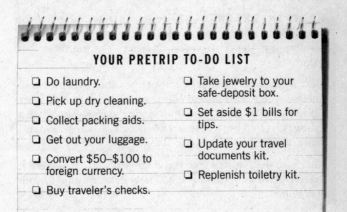

YOUR PRETRIP TO-DO LIST

❑ Do laundry.

❑ Pick up dry cleaning.

❑ Collect packing aids.

❑ Get out your luggage.

❑ Convert $50–$100 to foreign currency.

❑ Buy traveler's checks.

❑ Take jewelry to your safe-deposit box.

❑ Set aside $1 bills for tips.

❑ Update your travel documents kit.

❑ Replenish toiletry kit.

COLLECT PACKING HELPS The first thing to do is to start collecting packing helpers such as tissue paper, plastic dry-cleaning bags (your local cleaner may be willing to sell you as many as you need), and garbage bags.

HAUL OUT YOUR LUGGAGE Open your luggage and place it on the floor in your bedroom, so you can prepack items as you remember them. If you are using a new garment bag, experiment to discover which hangers work best with it. If you don't have the right ones, get them now.

DO LAST-MINUTE ERRANDS Convert enough foreign currency to allow you to hail a cab from the airport to your hotel and for tips to bellhops when you get there ($50 to $100 should do it—ask for small bills). Arrange to put most of your money into traveler's checks.

Begin setting aside $1 bills to use as tips while on the road—it saves having to struggle with minute amounts of an unfamiliar currency. Throughout the Caribbean and in many cruise ports as well as many places that are even farther afield, dollars are happily accepted. If you're traveling to Europe or Asia, however, it's better to deal in euros or yen from the get-go.

DROP IN ESSENTIALS Designate a specific place for your personal documents kit, and add your travel documents— passport, airline tickets, traveler's checks—as you remember them.

Tuck a generous handful of empty resealable bags into your suitcase, along with a large plastic or mesh bag to keep dirty clothes separate from clean ones along the way. Also, pack a lightweight tote bag to use as a day pack or to carry new purchases on the trip back home.

Check on the status of your travel kits (*see above*). Replenish toiletry items as needed, and add new items specific to your upcoming trip.

TEST RUN

A week or less before your trip, put all the things you intend to take into the suitcase you want to take it in, and spend about 20 minutes carrying it around. Walk around your house, go up and down your driveway, tackle some steps, heave it into your car trunk and pull it out again a couple of times. This replicates situations you'll encounter while you travel: going from your house or hotel to a car or taxi, or through train stations, and along city streets. Consider whether your suitcase will fit into the spaces you might encounter—trunks of compact cars, tiny rooms in old hotels and bed-and-breakfasts, and steep, curvy stairways in antique buildings. Remember that the wheels that serve you so well in an airport are practically useless on cobblestones, grassy paths, gravel walkways, and endless train-station staircases. If your suitcase is too heavy or awkward, start thinking about how you're going to cut back your wardrobe.

❯ The Night Before

No one is saying you should plan to pull an all-night packing session. But clothing does wrinkle and needs to breathe, so it's best to pack as close to your departure time as possible—your clothes will thank you.

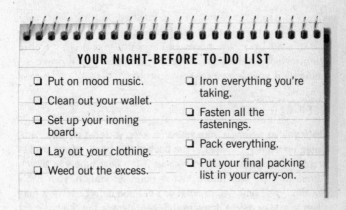

YOUR NIGHT-BEFORE TO-DO LIST

❑ Put on mood music.

❑ Clean out your wallet.

❑ Set up your ironing board.

❑ Lay out your clothing.

❑ Weed out the excess.

❑ Iron everything you're taking.

❑ Fasten all the fastenings.

❑ Pack everything.

❑ Put your final packing list in your carry-on.

GET IN THE MOOD Because packing can be stressful, you may wish to light some scented candles and listen to Chopin or Kenny G. Or you may prefer to crank up the Rolling Stones and knock back a long-neck bottle of beer. You may seek silence. You'll definitely need an ironing board.

EDIT, EDIT, EDIT Set up your ironing board near a large, flat space such as a tabletop or bed. (If your ironing board is your bed, that's another story.) Lay out all of the clothing you plan to take and look it over. Most packers claim that this is the critical moment, when you should remove half of the clothing and pack only the remaining half. You will do this a little less painfully if you have previously discovered how heavy and unwieldy your bag will be if you're forced to carry it for any length of time—as you eventually will be, almost certainly. Just keep refining your list, weeding out extras and single-use items. As you work with your assembled wardrobe, a certain logic—call it the Zen of Packing—will come to your aid and allow you to make the correct choices.

Try to stay focused not on what might possibly be useful, in a pinch, but instead on what you simply won't be able to live without.

One more pointer. When you've finished pruning down your list, cross off your last-minute deletions and slip a copy of the list in your briefcase, purse, or carry-on; give a copy to the friend who's holding down the fort at home. It will prove invaluable if your luggage is lost or stolen.

KEEP OLD LISTS

Once you've returned from your trip, keep your list on your computer, on a sheet of paper in the back of this book, or in a pocket of your luggage so you can consult it the next time you travel. Annotate it on your return, noting your destination, your trip's duration, and notes as to what you did and didn't use. You may need to add or delete items to suit the itinerary, but the basic list may well remain the same.

IRON EVERYTHING If you start out with a well-pressed piece, the chances of its creasing en route are, well, de-creased—no matter what the luggage or how long the trip. Ironed clothes also lie flatter and thus take up less space. (Hint: jeans that are ironed—or even better, dry-cleaned—pack into less space than jeans that have been merely laundered. They also look good longer.) Place ironed clothing on hangers until you are ready to fold.

BUTTON UP Fasten every button, zip every zipper, and hook every hook of your clothing. It makes all the difference for a shirt placket to lie for eight hours as God and Ralph Lauren intended, as opposed to being bent or folded unnaturally.

And now you're ready to pack.

Get Packing!

Once upon a time there were two women—college room-mates and fast friends—who agreed on almost everything except how to pack a suitcase. One was convinced that she could get more stuff in by spreading her clothes absolutely flat in the bottom of the case and folding it all together more or less simultaneously into a bundle; the other was a passionate devotee of the rolling-up school of thought. In college, they argued about this every time they packed their bags—every Christmas, every spring break, every June. And now, some 25 years later, they still argue about it every time they take their families to visit each other.

▶ How to Fill Almost Any Suitcase

The truth is, each type of garment can be folded in a different way, and each bag lends itself to a different method of packing. Even seemingly identical black roll-aboards can present a completely different mien inside, depending on what kind of compartments are inside and on whether the telescoping handles are mounted internally or externally. Different suitcases require a completely different approach.

If there are no compartments inside, you can pack as if there are, or even make your own divider. If the bottom of your suitcase is perfectly flat, start by laying flat items like an envelope of art prints or your portable office at the bottom. Then add a tight layer of irregularly shaped items such as rolled-up socks, topped by another layer made up of a bundle of clothing packed using the interlock method or stacks—your preference. For the easiest access to the bottom layer, one travel writer makes a horizontal divider from a piece of heavy cardboard (you could use poster board or Foam Core) trimmed to fit right into her suitcase; if you cut out hand holes on either side of this board, it's very easy to lift up the top layer to grab something from the bottom. (If your telescoping bag handles are mounted internally, put the flat items on top of the cardboard and rolled items on the bottom layer, fitted in around the handle structure.)

Does your bag have its own suiter? Or two entirely separate sections? Forget about the horizontal divider and either roll or interlock as you prefer. The following pages demonstrate the essential techniques you need to know—the "dressmaker's dummy," the "roll," and the "interlock"—to ensure a well-packed piece of luggage, whether it hangs, rolls, or rides on your back.

LAST IN, FIRST OUT

Whether you roll or fold or interlock, put the things you need first into your suitcase last. Arriving at the ski lodge late? Toss your family's PJs onto the top of the pile, right on top of the outfits you'll all need first thing in the morning. In this way, although it's generally a good idea to unpack as soon as you arrive at your hotel, you won't absolutely have to do so, and you can get started early and leave unpacking for later.

If you're packing a standard pullman by the stacking method, you can do the entire stack chronologically—the first day's outfit on top, the second day's clothes below that, and so forth. This will eliminate the need to paw through everything to unearth that purple polo shirt you meant to wear in the opening-day golf tournament.

ROCK AND ROLL Rolling is an easy way to pack clothing, both light and heavy. It works best for duffels and travel packs, but if your trip is casual, you can roll garments for standard suitcases as well.

Let's demonstrate with a T-shirt: Lay the shirt facedown on a flat surface. Fold in the sleeves. Then, with the shirt still facedown, begin to roll it up from the bottom hem. Smooth it as you go, so that no wrinkles are folded in. The collar should wind up on the outside of the roll.

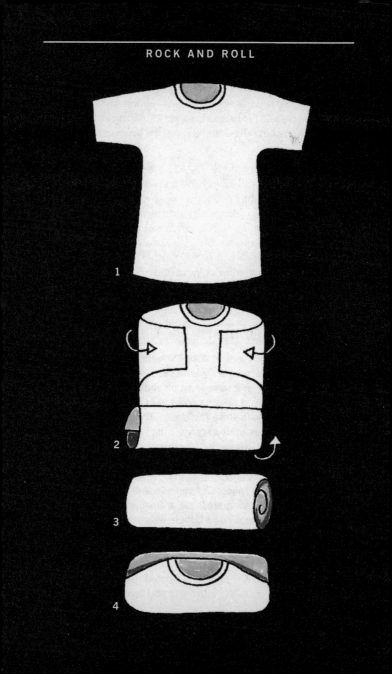

Jeans are a natural for this process. Even dress slacks can be rolled: hold them upside down, by the cuffs, and lay them out, then roll from the cuffs up. Bruce, who almost always packs in a travel pack, even rolls sports jackets: fold the jacket in half lengthwise, tucking the arms inside, then begin at the top and roll down.

Delicate garments should be placed on top of T-shirts or tissue paper before being rolled, jellyroll fashion. Even a garment as elaborate as a silk shirt or a piqué sundress can be rolled. Just fill the dress with a plastic dry-cleaning bag, backing and fronting it with two more bags, then roll it from the hem up. Skirts can be done this way as well. Put a plastic dry-cleaning bag inside the skirt to pad it, then either roll it, or fold it in half lengthwise over another garment to pad the crease, then roll. Having once rolled a plastic-encased garment, you'll swear that rolling rocks.

HOW SNUG IS TOO TIGHT?

It's the novice packer's nightmare, the very reason for this book. You carefully figure out your wardrobe, carefully lay everything into your suitcase—and have to sit on your suitcase lid to get it shut. Or, if it zips, you need to enlist help to hold the fabric together so that you can close the zipper. This kind of tight packing not only strains your luggage hinges or zipper, but also generates wrinkles. However, ultraloose packing is not much better. If your suitcase isn't full enough, the things inside will move around and crumple. Try to pack snugly so that your possessions just fill the space. Did you edit and prune so carefully that you have room to spare? Use a smaller piece of luggage, add a couple of items, or add bubble wrap as padding. You can use it to cushion purchases you make during your trip for the way home.

THE INTERLOCK The theory behind the interlock, which works best with standard suitcases and travel packs, is that each piece of clothing folds over or is cushioned by another piece. It's really quite simple: Lay a pair of slacks or a skirt

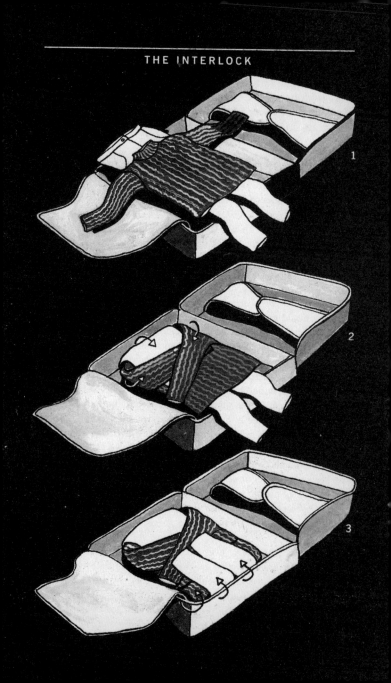

across an open suitcase from north to south, allowing any sur-
plus to drape over either end. Place a sweater from east to
west, allowing arms to drape both east and west and tail to
drape to the south. Keep on layering until you have run
through most of your clothes. Add your toilet kit and any
folded or rolled items. Now flip the northern part of the slacks
over the top of the sweater, fold the sweater arms in over this,
then fold the bottom of the sweater and the southern part of
the slacks or skirt over everything. You've created a neat stack
of clothing that provides cushioning everywhere a wrinkle
wants to be. You can add as few or as many garments to this
construction as you wish. When you're finished, fill in the corners and crevices with underwear, socks, scarves, etc.

USE YOUR SHOES!

Shoes should never be empty—they should always be stuffed
with underwear, socks, a child's shoe, a purse-size travel umbrella. Otherwise, the hollows of your shoes are just wasted
space, and those small items are free to wriggle into whatever
crevice they please. We all harbor fears that a customs official
will fling open our suitcase, revealing our Victoria's Secret teddy
or heart-dappled boxer shorts to the airport community at large;
stuff them in a shoe and he'll never notice. Depending on how
fancy you want to get, you can buy cloth drawstring shoe bags
or encase them in socks or in shower caps you've collected from
previous travels or stick them into plastic shopping bags, or plastic bags you've acquired in the produce department at the gro-
cery store, or plastic sandwich bags . . . you get the idea. But do
pack shoes separately rather than as a pair—they offer greater
positioning possibilities that way.

DOUBLE STACKS This is the way that most people put
clothing into their luggage. Fold your clothes, using the folding
techniques described below, then place them in the case in two
neat stacks. Fill in around the edges and in the center with underwear and socks, bathing suits, etc. If your suitcase has interior straps that you can use to secure clothing, use them.

When you pack clothing into a
pullman, you can fold and stack,
roll and stack, or use a
combination of these methods.

TRADE TISSUE PAPER FOR PLASTIC!

One of life's little injustices is that whether you fill a suitcase by
upending the contents of your dresser drawer into the main
compartment, or by folding and neatly laying things in, you will
have wrinkles. And whether they are the chaotic wrinkles that
mark a dumper or the organized wrinkles of someone who has
packed carefully, you'll lack that bandbox-fresh look that you'd
have at home. (In fact, you can end up with wrinkles even if a
garment bag is your luggage of choice.) Although some packing experts swear that tissue paper yields the most crease-free
packing, plastic is even better. (Why does it work? Partly because the thin cushion it provides prevents a sharp crease from
forming; partly because its slippery quality keeps a potential
fold in the fabric on the move so that the odd crease that does
form doesn't stay in one place long enough to set.)

So when trip time approaches, collect plastic dry-cleaner bags—
bags without writing on them, that is, since the ink can rub off.
You can save them or ask your cleaner to sell or give you several
dozen. (Most are happy to do so—and a whole roll will last you a
lifetime.) Then, use them liberally for everything that you want to
roll, fold, or hang wrinkle-free.

Folding or rolling? Either way, to stave off wrinkling, lay plastic
underneath and on top of a garment before you fold or roll it.

Traveling with a garment bag? Start with a hanger with an
empty dry-cleaner bag over it. Add a dress. Then top it with a
second dry-cleaner bag. If you want, you can make this ensemble the base of a dressmaker's dummy (*see below*). Each time
you add a new garment, either add another plastic bag or use
each garment to pad the next—pull shirt sleeves through vest
armholes, for example.

Packing in a duffel or pullman? Put a plastic bag inside and outside
wrinkle-prone clothing to provide extra padding. You might do the
dressmaker's dummy with plastic for business clothing—and then
roll the package into a bundle and throw it into your duffel.

Let's hear it for plastic.

When you pack clothing into a pullman, you can fold and stack, roll and stack, or use a combination of these methods.

Alternatively, you can roll your clothes and then stack them neatly like cigarettes in a box. Again, if you lay them in so that the things you plan to wear first are on top, you'll have the easiest time getting to your gear.

▶ For Duffels and Travel Packs

The challenge with duffels and travel packs is twofold: the soft-side construction and the large single compartment. There is little to keep clothing from being squashed, and items can become disorganized and sometimes even "lost" in the bottom. Often you have to unpack and repack to get at small items. There are two ways to prevent this. One is to perfect the "roll" for clothing (*see above*). The other is to investigate travel organizers that effectively partition the space so that items remain in place and are protected.

EASY ACCESS

Stick your reading material in the pack's outside pockets—not only so that you can easily reach it en route, but also so that it will provide a hard shell to protect your clothing.

THE KEY—DISTRIBUTE THE WEIGHT After rolling all your clothing, give some thought to how you plan to carry your luggage. With a duffel, since you usually use a shoulder strap or top handles, pack your heaviest items, such as shoes and your toiletries kit, if you won't need it right away, on the bottom. Then put in your rolls of clothing, either horizontally or vertically. Remember to put the stuff you plan to use first on top.

To fill travel packs, most people lay them down like a standard suitcase. But then, when on one's back, where they are usually carried, everything will tend to slip out of place. Remember this simple fact when you pack, and start the process by standing your pack up in a chair so that it looks more like a shelf.

THE ZONE SYSTEM As mentioned above, the large central space of a duffel or pack can be a real problem when it comes to smaller items. Hunting for lost black socks, which finally turn up in the bottom of a black duffel, is no way to spend 20 minutes of your vacation time. Veteran duffel travelers keep things organized via a sort of zone system, using mesh bags of all sizes, either specialized packing folders sold in luggage accessory stores or mesh laundry bags made for sweaters, lingerie, and other delicate items. The mesh bags dry quickly when wet, allow air to get at the clothes when it's hot, and are see-through enough so you can find what you're looking for pretty quickly. Some people like to use gallon-size or two-gallon-size plastic resealable bags or zippered plastic blanket bags (you can buy them in housewares stores if you don't have any around the house). You might choose a different bag for each clothing type; all the socks go into one bag, all the shirts go into another, etc. Once everything is sorted, throw all the bags into your duffel and get going. When you need something, you can find it quickly, and barely disturb anything else. During the trip, you can re-sort what's in the bags to keep dirty laundry separate from clean stuff.

▶ Know-How for Garment Baggers

The advantage of a garment bag is that your clothes can be kept neatly on hangers, ready to transfer to a hotel closet. But because these bags are soft-sided and don't have much of a frame, clothes are easily crushed and creased in them. Shrewd packing can reduce this problem.

YOUR BASIC HANG-UPS Items fresh from the dry cleaner can go straight into the garment bag. When hanging a single garment on a hanger, first place a dry-cleaning bag over the hanger. This will protect the garment from resting directly on the hanger as well as provide a little stuffing, or cushioning, to help keep the garment's shape. Add garment, stuff sleeves with tissue paper if needed, then encase in plastic. (Note: The plastic bag traps air, which will help to cushion this garment from the one you'll place on top of it. Although you may pack a garment bag vertically, it does not remain that way; once the bag is closed, folded, and stowed, items lie directly on top of one another.) Does one stubborn garment keep slipping off the hanger? Try securing it with clothespins or straight pins, taking care to pin on an unseen part of the garment, to prevent crimping.

FROM TIES TO TIARAS

Some men prefer to roll ties up and put them in shoes. Others buy nifty tie-holder cases. (C'mon, guys, these add weight!) Other options that work: roll them and slip them into a jacket pocket. Lay them flat inside the sleeve of a jacket, then fold the jacket. Or take a piece of cardboard the length of the tie and roll the tie around it; secure with a rubber band. If you're packing in a garment bag, you can simply drape your ties over a padded hanger bar. Still other men go with bow ties—they're easier to pack.

Traveling with your tiara? One Fodor's staffer, whose resume includes a stint accompanying Miss America on a publicity tour, shares the beauty queen's secret of packing the prize headgear: Wrap the tiara in a silk scarf, drop it into an appropriately sized coffee can, affix lid, and go. (The Martha Stewarts among us will surely spray paint that coffee tin a brilliant gold.)

Sequined outfits can be protected with plastic inside and out before folding, or simply turned inside out and folded or rolled, then protected inside a resealable plastic bag.

As for your jewelry, earrings or studs and cuff links can go into small 35mm-film canisters—drop these into the pocket of your tux or into the evening bag you've planned to take on the big night. Alternatively, you might stick the posts of pierced-ear earrings through a square of felt, velvet, or Ultrasuede, then roll the whole thing up and tie it with a ribbon. Some travelers put all their jewelry into a molded eyeglass case. Bulky beads can go into snack-size resealable plastic bags.

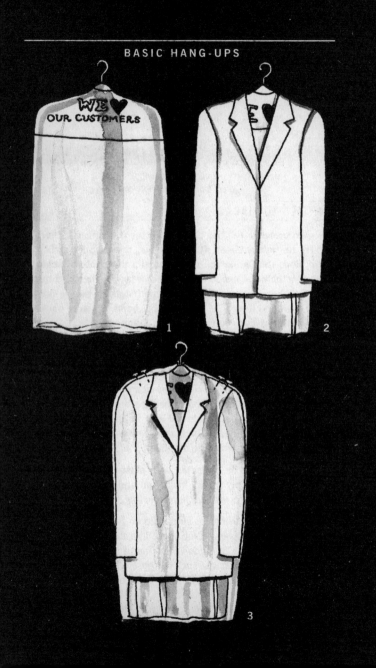

THE DRESSMAKER'S DUMMY Veteran packers know this technique can maximize the clothing you pack with a minimum of hangers, while cutting down on creases. Begin with a bare hanger. Put a T-shirt over it. Add a dress. Pull the arms of the T-shirt through the arms of the dress. Cover with a vest, sweater, or jacket. (Try to plan it so that these various pieces actually make up one real outfit. This way, you can save time when unpacking and just grab a single hanger.) Encase in a dry-cleaning bag. If you are packing pants, use a hanger with a padded bar, or pad the bar of the hanger with a T-shirt or sweater, so that you don't put too sharp a crease in your trousers when you drape them over the bar. (Tie technique #1: add a matching tie now, draping it over your slacks.) Cover with a long-sleeve shirt, then add a jacket. Pull the sleeves of the shirt through the jacket sleeves. (Tie technique #2: roll up a matching tie, then slip it into your jacket pocket.) You can also do the dressmaker's dummy outfit by outfit; group coordinating accessories for each one in a resealable plastic bag; then poke a hole in the bag to slip it over the top of the hanger. Encase all in plastic, and proceed to next outfit.

KEEP IT CREASE-FREE It's a good idea to hang the longest garments in the bag first, then follow with the shorter ones, and put the wrinkle-prone items behind (or underneath) those that are wrinkleproof. This way, when the tails of the longer garments are folded to fit into the bag, they are cushioned by the hems of the shorter garments, and the clothes that resist wrinkles pad the fold of the ones that wrinkle, preventing a crease. To prevent a crease, you can also pad the fold with nonwrinkling items such as underwear, socks, or bathing suits. Hang delicate items in the middle of the bag, not in the front or back, so that they are not wrinkled when the bag is closed and folded in half. To really rout wrinkles, you can hang each item over a plastic dry-cleaning bag and encase the garment in a second dry-cleaning bag. Before closing the bag, fill any empty corners with rolled-up socks, sweaters, and other

small items to prevent shifting. Then lay two more dry-cleaning bags over the clothing to protect against crimping from the internal straps.

SHOES IN GARMENT BAGS Most heavy-duty garment bags have inside compartments for shoes and other gear. If you're taking high-heel, pointy dress pumps, be sure to wrap them in a cushioning material, to spare your bag a puncture wound.

HANDY TRAVEL ACCESSORIES Look for a hanging organizer with a fabric back and see-through plastic pockets, similar to an oversize jewelry roll. This is ideal for panty hose, scarves, slips, and other items. The hook on top allows you to hang it in the garment bag as well as in your hotel closet. The see-through plastic saves you time spent searching for things.

If you are using regular hangers rather than the ones that came with your bag, use a twist-tie to keep the hangers together.

A luggage strap cinched around the middle of the bag gives you extra assurance that your bag won't come open when the baggage handlers toss it into the plane or haul it out. Twist-ties, a knot of dental floss, a paper clip, or a small safety pin discourage casual investigation, in lieu of closing every compartment with a lock.

WHAT NOT TO PACK Never pack toiletries in a garment bag you plan to check. There is simply too much risk of the bag being mishandled, causing all kinds of leaks and spillage. Bring toiletries on board the airplane. If you must pack them in your checked garment bag, line the compartment with a plastic bag. Then keep your fingers crossed.

And don't place anything of value in the outside pockets of your garment bag, unless they lock. This is a good place for books, shoes, socks, and other mundane items that would give a thief an instant case of ennui.

▶ Practically Crease-Free Folding

No matter what kind of luggage you use, the time eventually comes when you'll need to fold something—perhaps even the dreaded long-sleeve Oxford-cloth shirt. Using a few tried-and-true methods, you can keep wrinkling to a minimum. If you're really compulsive or if looking wrinkle-free matters, you will button everything around an empty plastic dry-cleaning bag (you can even thread these long plastic bags through the sleeves) and then put a plastic bag on top of the garment before you fold it.

ONCE IN YOUR HOTEL ROOM

Try to unpack as completely as possible as soon as possible so your clothing has a chance to breathe and wrinkles can fall out naturally. Let's say that you plan to change hotels every night for six nights and are using a garment bag. The minute you get to the room, remove only what you need for the evening and the following morning. Even this small amount of breathing room will cut down on last-minute pressing.

TOPS: THE CLOTHING-STORE METHOD At a well-known nationwide casual clothing chain that shall remain nameless, long-sleeve button-down shirts are folded in the following way: Button all the buttons, including the top-collar button. Place the shirt facedown on a flat surface. Bring in the left side of the shirt body about 2 or 3 inches and fold. Take the arm and fold it straight down, parallel to the shirt body, with the cuff at the shirttail; line up the outer edge of the arm with the edge of the shirt body. Do the same for the right side. Bring the shirttail section up a third of the way, then fold over again, so that when you turn the shirt over, the collar is on top.

TOPS: THE DRY-CLEANER METHOD You, too, can master the tricks of the neighborhood dry-cleaning wizard and his folding machine. And unlike most television stunts, you actually can try this at home. Begin as directed above: Button the buttons and lay the shirt facedown. Then, without bending the shirt body, bring the left arm of the shirt to lie horizontally across the top back of the shirt, so that you're creasing it at the shoulder joint. Do the same with the right sleeve. (If sleeves are longer than the body of the shirt is wide, try folding each sleeve in at the cuff.) Fold the left side of the shirt in about 2 or 3 inches, then fold the right side. Bring shirttail section up a third of the way, then fold over again, so that when you turn the shirt over, the collar is on top. Although this method requires a few extra folds, and folds have a way of becoming creases, many men insist that this is their favorite method. Most don't actually fold the shirts themselves; it's just easier to pack a shirt when it's fresh from the dry cleaner.

TOPS: THE STACK-AND-FOLD METHOD Stack several buttoned shirts atop one another, facedown on a flat surface, and proceed to fold them all as one: Bend the left arm at the shoulder joint and bring it down to lie parallel with the shirt body, cuff touching shirttail. Do the same with the right arm. Then bring the shirttail up to meet the collar.

ESPECIALLY FOR LONG-SLEEVE SWEATERS Put your sweater facedown on a flat surface. Bending the sweater only at the shoulder joint, fold the arms in to lie horizontally across the top back of the sweater. Then bring the bottom up to meet the top.

HOW TO FOLD SLACKS Lay slacks on a flat surface and line up the legs so that the center creases meet, both in front and in back. Bring the outer leg halfway up so that the corner of the outer cuff touches the back pocket, and bring the inner leg up to align with the front pocket (this eliminates some bulk). You can then fold the slacks in half again.

THE CLOTHING STORE METHOD

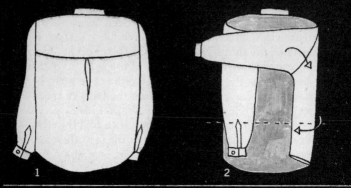

1

2

THE DRY-CLEANER METHOD

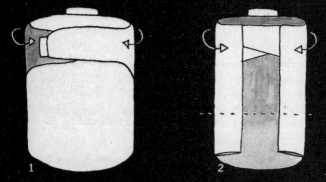

1

2

THE STACK-AND-FOLD METHOD

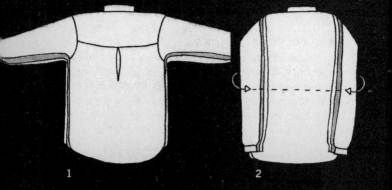

1

2

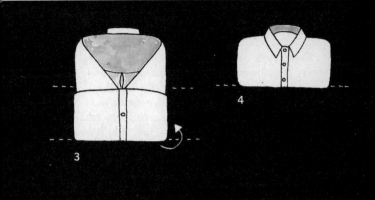

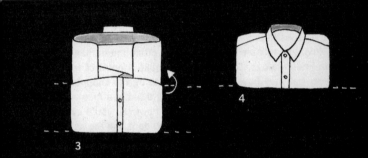

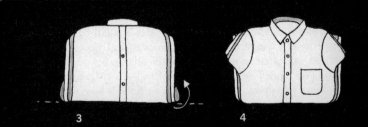

▌About Your Carry-Ons

If you plan to pack everything you need for your trip into a cabin carry-on, efficient packing techniques are really important: check out the roll method and the interlock. If your under-the-seat carry-on is soft-sided, it's a good idea to lay any books or magazines you've brought for in-flight reading on top—they're easier to reach that way, and they'll create an extra layer of protection for your gear when you shove your bag under the seat in front of you.

HOW TO PACK A SUN HAT

Some people prefer to bring their sun hats with them; after all, there's no substitute for a hat that you love, especially if it's one of the foldable, rollable models that you often find in mail order and on-line catalogs. Other travelers make a point of leaving whatever hat they have at home, trips being the shopping opportunity that they are. After all, buying a hat is a nice way to support the local economy. Either way, however, you'll eventually need to pack the hat. This is how you do it: Fill the hat with clothing, perhaps underwear and socks. Place the hat in the suitcase brim down. Tuck rolled clothing around the brim. Fill the suitcase around and over the hat. It will have been padded enough to retain its shape.

THE HEAVYWEIGHTS Plan to reserve heavy articles for your under-the-seat bag rather than the one you'll be stowing overhead. Compartment doors do occasionally pop open midflight, and weighty items increase the chance of your bag's toppling out (possibly onto your own head—ouch!). Even if that doesn't happen, you don't want to hoist a heavy load over your head to get it into (and out of) the compartment in the first place.

ANTICIPATING SECURITY CHECKPOINTS If you are carrying a laptop in a black case or other item that's not distinctive looking, make it unique. Tie a bandanna or colored ribbon around the handle, or stick a strip of fluorescent duct tape to each side. If you are detained for a body check after you go through the metal detector, you may not be able to grab your carry-ons the minute they emerge from the X-ray machine. There's always the possibility that someone else will retrieve your black laptop case rather than his own out of the logjam of personal belongings—whether by mistake or by design.

If you are bringing presents in your carry-on luggage, leave them unwrapped. Then, if they need to be examined at security checkpoints, your wrapping job won't have to be undone.

If you are carrying a syringe because of a medical condition being treated by injections, have the medication in your pharmacy's packaging and bring a copy of the prescription.

Safety razors and tweezers are permitted. So are nail clippers, provided they are without the attached metal nail file. Umbrellas and walking canes will be inspected to make sure they conceal no weapons.

WHAT IF YOU HAVE TO CHECK A CARRY-ON?
In anticipation of being forced to gate-check your carry-on, either because it doesn't fit or because all overheads are full, always prepare your carry-on as though you might have to check it—label it, flag it with a ribbon or tape to make it stand out, lock it, and remove anything that doesn't belong in checked luggage. (Alternatively, segregate items you absolutely must have on board into one part of your suitcase, because you don't want to be rummaging for your carry-on must-haves in full view of half your fellow passengers.) Then, when you end up bringing home an extra shopping tote packed with a plaster-of-paris copy of the Parthenon (complete with three-dimensional centaurs in the pediments), you can check your original carry-on bag with some peace of mind.

CARRY-ON MUSTS

- ❏ Baby wipes
- ❏ Business papers and manuscripts
- ❏ Camera, breakables
- ❏ CD or tape player, tapes or CDs
- ❏ Change of clothes and a swimsuit
- ❏ Diaper bag
- ❏ DVDs, DVD player, extra batteries
- ❏ Exposed film
- ❏ Eyeglasses, sunglasses
- ❏ Food to eat in flight
- ❏ Gifts
- ❏ Jewelry, heirlooms, valuables
- ❏ Keys
- ❏ Laptop, extra battery, diskettes
- ❏ Money, foreign currency, credit cards
- ❏ Packing list
- ❏ Paper and pen
- ❏ Personal documents kit
- ❏ Prescription medications
- ❏ Reading material, guidebook
- ❏ Receipts
- ❏ Small toiletries kit
- ❏ Sweater
- ❏ Water (eight ounces per flight hour)

FOR OVERNIGHT FLIGHTS, ADD:

- ❏ Neck pillow
- ❏ Sleep mask, earplugs
- ❏ Soft slippers or warm socks
- ❏ Spare eyeglasses, lens case and supplies

NEVER CHECK THIS STUFF Even if you're checking other bags, you'll probably also be taking a carry-on into the passenger cabin with you. Among other things, it should always include anything breakable or too valuable or important to consign to the cargo hold—such as jewelry and valuables, items of sentimental value, prescription medications, your

CARRY-ON NO-NOS

- ❏ Baseball bats
- ❏ Billy clubs, brass knuckles
- ❏ Cigar cutters
- ❏ Corkscrews, bottle openers
- ❏ Darts
- ❏ Golf clubs
- ❏ Guns, gunpowder, ammunition
- ❏ Hairspray (large cans)
- ❏ Helium balloons
- ❏ Hockey sticks, hockey skates
- ❏ Ice picks
- ❏ Ice skates
- ❏ Knitting needles and crochet hooks
- ❏ Knives, plastic as well as metal
- ❏ Letter openers
- ❏ Metal nail files
- ❏ Pool cues
- ❏ Razor blades
- ❏ Scissors with pointed tips
- ❏ Screwdrivers
- ❏ Ski poles
- ❏ Tennis rackets
- ❏ Toy guns, water pistols, fake guns
- ❏ Weapons, including Mace, tear gas, pepper spray
- ❏ Anything that could leak and generate toxic fumes

spare pair of eyeglasses, plane tickets or e-ticket flight confirmations, tour vouchers, photocopies of your travel documents, business documents, receipts for recent purchases you've packed in checked luggage, photo equipment, and personal photos. Your entire personal documents kit should travel with you as well.

Some of the souvenirs or gifts you'll buy during your trip will fall into the "valuables" category. Plan to have more room in your carry-on for the return trip than you did coming out.

Less obviously, it's a good idea to put in any gifts you've brought for whoever's meeting you at your destination. You'll also want to have in-flight reading material as well as any in-flight travel accessories you want to use—neck pillow, a sleeping mask, slippers, etc.

ANTICIPATE PROBLEMS Pack a change of clothing, just in case your luggage gets lost—or something gets spilled all over you during the flight. (Turbulence happens, and so do clumsy flight attendants.)

And if your destination is the Caribbean or some other sunny spot or a hotel with a pool anywhere, why not add your bathing suit—it's light and takes up very little space. If, say, you've landed in Jamaica but your checked luggage hasn't, what do you care, if you've got your bathing suit? Go and bask on a luscious bit of beach or splash around in the pool while your bags are being found.

If your trip is in a busy travel season or if the weather nationwide looks threatening, it's especially important to carry extras of things you may need—extra contact lens supplies, an extra day or two of prescription medication, extra food and drink, extra diversions for your journey—in case you're rerouted or delayed.

MAKE YOURSELF COMFORTABLE The air inside the cabin is as dry as desert air. The humidity level can be as low as 2%—quite a change from the 50% level most people consider comfortable. Drinking alcohol or coffee, both diuretics, can compound the effect. As a result, dehydration is common, and it can throw your whole body out of whack.

To counteract the dry cabin air, it's smart to bring your own water—at least eight ounces for every hour you're in the air. Drinking continuously will keep you hydrated and so you'll be less exhausted when you land, and your skin won't have that parched feeling that usually lingers after a long flight. You can't assume you will be able to get an adequate supply of water from the crew, because airlines often don't carry enough for everyone, and in any case, you may not be able to get the attention of the flight attendant when you want to take a sip. While you're sleeping, you can stash your bottle right next to you so that you can take a swig every time you wake up. (Freeze your bottle before you leave home and your water supply will be constantly chilled.)

Bring a small spray bottle and you can spritz your face with water to keep it from feeling too dry. Moisturizer and lotion are also essential.

BYO FOOD Although you will have checked with the airline about in-flight food service during your earlier research, do consider that turbulence and delays could push a planned meal service long past the time that you're ready to eat. If the airline had not planned to feed you, you could also go for many hours without the chance to get a bite, what with waiting in line before boarding and sitting at the gate or on the tarmac before you take off and after you land; you may not have the time to stop at an airport concession before you take off.

If you had planned to buy food at the airport between connecting flights, you may find that the concessions are all outside security checkpoints—and you may not have the time to reclear security. Or you may have to reclear security just to get to your next flight, and the waiting game there may eat up the time you'd planned to use to buy something at the concession stand. Or you may have time to make the purchase—but not to stand in the line to make your request. Because so few passengers are being fed in flight, many people are looking for meals at airport food outlets. All this is a long way of saying that bringing food to the airport is usually a very smart move.

FOOD IDEAS You can prepare your food in your own kitchen or pick up a meal to go en route to the airport. Smaller items are better; think crackers, nuts, popcorn, sliced raw vegetables, fresh or dried fruit, small sandwiches. Soup and stew are good, but only if you have a leakproof plastic thermos. Just-add-water-and-eat soups in their own cardboard containers are lightweight and filling. Stay away from soupy dishes packed in containers that might leak or spill. And you may want to consider whether crunchy foods that generate a lot of crumbs, such as baguettes, are worth the mess. Smelly foods such as tuna fish may disturb other passengers. Dried-cocoa packets are good. For dessert, add yogurt, a cookie, or fruit—an apple, pear, or orange, or sliced strawberries in a small plastic container. You can put each individual meal in a gallon- or quart-size resealable plastic bag, accompanied by plastic forks and spoons, small paper plates, and plenty of napkins; if you bring a beverage, it should be in a plastic bottle, since some airlines do not permit glass containers of any kind on board. Finally, if you need to slice or chop anything, do it at home. Preslice bread, spread spreadables, and cut fruit and cheese beforehand. No knives, even plastic ones, can be brought through security checkpoints.

A WORD ABOUT COURTESY The carry-on concept may have begun after Amy Vanderbilt and Emily Post had their say, but as more travelers opt to carry their luggage aboard and as airlines continue to cut back on the size of overhead compartments and underseat legroom, your fellow passengers will thank you for observing a few heretofore unwritten rules of carry-on etiquette.

Most important, remember that one overhead compartment serves two and sometimes three passengers. Try to fit your things into the smallest possible space, to leave room for your fellow passengers' gear. By all means cooperate if flight attendants need to rearrange bags or move them to accommodate more carry-ons on a crowded flight. You'll depart that much faster if everyone is flexible.

If you are asked to check your luggage after boarding, do cooperate with the flight attendant. Most likely, he or she has asked you to do so because your luggage really is too large, or perhaps because the flight is full. You will have anticipated this situation, right?

Savvy Checking

Consigning your suitcase containing your favorite clothing to an airline is something of an act of faith. You've heard the horror stories. Still, millions of bags are transported uneventfully every year, and of those that don't come off the airplane as they're supposed to, almost all of them are reunited with their owners within 24 hours. A little knowledge goes a long way, however. A few simple precautions can help your luggage stay on track, and you can improve on the odds of getting it back (or getting your due from the airline if you don't).

WHAT'S IT WORTH TO YOU? The first thing you need to know are your rights. For lost or damaged bags in the United States, airlines are liable for up to only $2,500 per passenger. That's double the limit that was in place until 2000, but skimpy compared with the replacement costs of a suitcase full of nice clothing. But even these limits are higher than those on international flights. On these a treaty known as the Warsaw Convention sets the airline's liability limit at a maximum $9.07 per pound. To determine the amount, the airline either weighs your bags at check-in and notes the amount on your ticket; or it assumes that each of your bags weighs the maximum allowed for baggage, about 70 pounds apiece, giving you a maximum of about $640 per bag. This limit applies both on completely international flights and on domestic segments of an overseas journey; if you begin your trip in Cleveland, change planes in New York, and continue to Paris, and if your bag gets lost in New York, the loss will be covered under the less generous international rules. Whatever you say about the value of your possessions, airlines typically argue that the depreciated value is operative rather than the replacement cost.

PROTECT YOURSELF One way to get around the limits is to purchase what's known as "excess valuation" coverage, when it's available. (It may not be for international flights.) It

TIPS FROM AN ANONYMOUS BAGGAGE HANDLER

Luggage truly takes a beating. It gets slammed into a dirty taxi trunk, thrown down onto the pavement in front of the airport terminal, then tossed onto a conveyor belt headed straight for . . . you guessed it, the baggage handlers. Ever wonder what life is really like behind those partitions? So here's the word from the guys themselves:

- "Buy soft-sided luggage. Hard-sided luggage tends to split open when thrown—excuse me, dropped—onto baggage carts and conveyor belts. Soft-sided luggage can take impact better."

- "Stay within airline limits on weight, size, etc. If your luggage is heavier than it should be, you may fool the ticket agent, but we bagmen will not thank you for it, and your poor luggage will surely pay."

- "Sorry, folks, but sometimes all a piece of luggage has to do is to look different—either in color, height, or size—to be singled out for abuse."

- "Bags that 'misbehave' are definitely going to get it. I have actually heard an associate of mine explain, 'The duffel got mean with me, so I got mean back.' "

- "Label all your luggage with your name and telephone number, both inside and out. Outside luggage tags are the first casualties."

- "While you're at it, pull off all those old luggage tags from your last trip. It really frosts me when people complain about a misdirected suitcase when there are tags for three different airports on the handle."

- "If your suitcase has detachable handles or straps, take them off before you check in. Some of my guys collect them and use 'em as dog leashes."

never covers valuable and breakable objects, so if you are carrying items such as antiques, musical instruments, jewelry, manuscripts, or negotiable securities, or large amounts of cash, you should buy your own insurance in advance in case the airline exercises its right to refuse to take on the additional responsibility. Also, if a check-in agent is concerned that your cargo may not survive the trip, he or she may ask you to sign a waiver stating that you're checking it at your own risk. That doesn't get the airline totally off the hook. Extensive exterior damage when you retrieve your bag could be considered as evidence of airline negligence, and you might be recompensed. Usually excess valuation costs $1 to $2 for every $100 of coverage. Also see if your home-owner's or renter's insurance policy covers losses away from home. Many do. And look into optional or automatic supplemental baggage coverage available through credit-card companies. Travel agencies and travel-insurance companies also sell baggage policies.

DON'T LOSE IT You don't have much control over whether your suitcase arrives right on time. But you have some. Make sure your suitcases are tagged correctly, for the right flight, the right airport, and the right airline for your itinerary. Know your destinations' airport codes before you get to your departure airport and make sure the tag that the check-in agent puts on your bag has the right airport code.

One good strategy: ask the skycap what the abbreviation stands for—even if you already know it. This will ensure that *he* is paying attention. Some of these airport codes are easy to decipher, such as Pittsburgh (PIT), Las Vegas (LAS), Denver (DEN), and London Heathrow (LHR). But others are less immediately obvious: Los Angeles (LAX), New Orleans (MSY), Hartford (BDL), Kalamazoo/Battle Creek (AZO), Nashville (BNA), Burlington, Vermont (BTV), and Orlando, Florida (MCO). One wrong letter and your suitcase may end up in Oman (MCT).

In addition, remove and discard tags left over from previous flights. Baggage-handlers won't be lingering over your suitcase to try to figure out which of the five tags on your bag is for today's trip.

TOP 10 CHECKED-LUGGAGE TIPS

- ❏ Find out the restrictions for all your flights; pack for the most restrictive.

- ❏ Buy excess valuation if appropriate.

- ❏ Make your luggage distinctive.

- ❏ Never overpack.

- ❏ ID your suitcases outside and in.

- ❏ Tear off old baggage tags.

- ❏ See that your airports' three-letter codes go on your new tags.

- ❏ Ask the skycap what the code means.

- ❏ Don't lose your claim checks.

- ❏ Don't leave the airport without reporting problems.

LOCK IT Although no luggage lock is 100% effective, locking your bags may deter thieves and, in any event, helps keep the latches from popping open. Many suitcases come with locks; if yours don't, you can buy them, either key-operated or with combinations. With the latter you get the advantage of having no keys to lose. In a pinch, you can hook small safety pins through the loops on your zipper pulls as a deterrent. Or, instead, use paper clips, plastic cable ties from electronics stores such as Radio Shack, or twist-ties; even the smallest barrier is sometimes enough to stop a thief who's short on time. If your luggage comes with keys, put them on your key chain so they don't get lost.

TAKE YOUR TAGS Get baggage stubs for each bag you check. Hang onto your tags until you've unpacked and confirmed that nothing is amiss. They are essential when the time comes to reclaim your bag, particularly one that has gone astray.

KNOW YOUR RESPONSIBILITIES If you are changing planes en route, make sure your bag will be checked through to your final destination. Ask about any unusual procedures. For example, if you are preclearing U.S. Customs at your connecting airport—say, on a Vancouver-Toronto–New York routing—you'd clear customs in Toronto, and you might need to reclaim your bag in Toronto, take care of the formalities, and then recheck the bag.

Finally, remove straps and hooks. These can get caught in baggage-processing machinery.

BRINGING SPECIAL CARGO?

It used to be permissible to carry on all kinds of large objects: portable cribs, big backpacks, golf bags, skis, skateboards, snowboards, and musical instruments. You still can carry aboard many of these items, but you must check with the airline in advance if you plan to do so. Most airlines let you bring aboard an item if it meets the same size restrictions imposed on other carry-ons. If you do not want to check a fragile or valuable item, say, a cello or other unwieldy object, many airlines permit you to buy an extra ticket and place it on the seat next to you. The protocol for checking sports gear—whether it's a bicycle, bowling ball, set of golf clubs, fishing pole, skis, or a snowboard—differs from one airline to the next, so check in advance and plan to ship the stuff if you have to.

CLOSE IT Don't stuff so much into your suitcase that you have to sit on it to get it closed. Overpacking strains the latches, the hinges, and the zipper, and weakens them over time. So abused, even sturdy luggage can pop open when it's not supposed to. When overstuffing is essential, a few layers of strapping tape or duct tape in strategic places are in order, depending on your suitcase. But remember that some airlines exclude liability for damages involving overstuffed suitcases.

4

HOW TO PACK
FOR THE WAY BACK

"To ship to the United States, that will be $70," the salesclerk says. There you are at Lladrós "R" Us in Toledo, Spain, and you've just negotiated a great price for a delicate Lladró figurine. Then, when you ask about shipping, you almost reconsider. But before you know it, you hear yourself saying, "No, thanks. I'll carry it myself." Unfortunately, by the time you're out the door, it's too late to change your mind. And it's just the second day of a two-week train trip in Europe, and you regret your purchase—and your decision not to ship the thing—for the rest of your journey. You breathe a sigh of relief when you finally unpack, back home, and find it undamaged. Had your lovely Lladró broken en route, you would have had no recourse.

Whether you're traveling for business or pleasure, the odds are you're going to accumulate material of one kind or another. Having a strategy for dealing with it is a wise idea and will make your return trip easier.

▶ Use Your Packing List

Here's hoping you followed the advice in Chapters 2 and 3 to write down your packing list and keep a copy. (And you did remember to cross off all those items you wisely decided at the last minute to leave at home, didn't you?) If you did, repacking should be a no-sweat process. By checking each item off the list as it is packed, you reduce the risk of leaving your favorite black all-season trousers behind.

This is especially useful if you've been staying in one place for a number of days—getting settled usually involves dispersing your belongings in various drawers and closets. And if you're traveling with a family, you can't count on your memory to make sure you've retrieved every little car and animal from under the beds, let alone make sure your child's beloved stuffed friend isn't hidden among the blankets.

Even if you've been changing hotels daily, virtually living out of your suitcase, double-checking the list is a good way to streamline the constant packing.

▶ Dirty Laundry

There's one major difference between the clothes you brought with you and the clothes you're taking home. On your return trip, most of your clothes will be dirty. That is, if you didn't pack way too many extra outfits. (If you did, remember this next time you get ready for a trip.)

Experienced travelers often bring a laundry bag, even if it's only a plastic trash bag, to keep the clothes they've already worn separate from fresh clothes. For long trips, count on a few visits to the Laundromat, or use hotel laundry services to get more wear out of your travel wardrobe. If you'll be using a Laundromat, bring a laundry bag strong enough to tote your dirty duds securely.

PACK BACKWARD

Do away with the last-minute rush to repack. Just take everything out of your suitcase on arrival, and put it back in as you wear it.

Remember how hard you had to work back home to fit everything into your suitcase in the first place? Balled-up dirty laundry will not occupy the same suitcase space as your carefully folded, rolled, or interlocked clean clothes. So dump out that dirty laundry and spread it flat, one piece at a time, in a stack in the bottom of your suitcase—if you've got a duffel you may want to reroll it—tightly, since you no longer have to worry about wrinkling. Around the corners tuck your shoes, stuffed with dirty socks and underwear. (Use shoe bags even though your clothes are dirty, or risk stains from any grease or tar that may be on the soles.) Break out those extra plastic bags you packed and bundle up anything that's damp so that it doesn't generate mildew in the rest of your clothing. Put the laundry bag on top, and then pack your remaining clothes. This procedure keeps clean and soiled stuff separate; when you get home, whatever is clean can go straight into your dresser or closet while the rest heads for the laundry hamper.

If you're repacking a garment bag, of course, you'll have to hang up your dirty clothes. If possible, put them in the front of the bag, where they will cushion your clean garments and help keep them from wrinkling. Use any remaining plastic dry-cleaner bags to separate clean and dirty garments.

▶ The Paper Chase

Few travelers understand the weight of paper in quite the way a travel journalist does. A single morning of hotel site inspections often yields six or eight hefty press kits; the paper accumulated during a five-day jaunt could fill an extra suitcase. And yet there's always the possibility that one of those brochures or releases will contain the pertinent fact that makes an article sing. What's a writer to do?

This same problem is shared by many business travelers. Conference materials, marketing reports, and brochures collected on the trade-show floor all have a way of stacking up on the desk in your hotel room.

KEEP IT UNDER CONTROL Try to consolidate the pile daily, even if it means staying awake an extra half hour each evening to do so. Discard exterior folders, and weed out duplicate information. Leaf through any particularly bulky documents to digest whatever sections are pertinent to you; tear out only the relevant pages, or jot down on a sheet of hotel stationery any facts you may need to retrieve later, so you can throw away the document. Or take notes and put them on your laptop or electronic organizer.

SHIP IT HOME If the pile is really huge, see if you can ship it. Some travelers mail (or express mail) printed material home to the office or house. Here's where the 10" x 13" manila envelopes in your portable office come in handy. Some travelers keep in touch with their office while on vacation by having a continual flow of paperwork sent via overnight mail; if you plan to do this, come equipped with filled-out overnight-mail vouchers so that you can wing the whole batch back to your desk at the end of the trip.

If your load is bulky but not as heavy as, say, papers and books, a trip to the local post office or express courier should suffice. Often your hotel can advise you on where to find shipping, or even handle it for you for a fee.

SCHLEP IT HOME If shipping isn't possible, you have only one option: carry it. If, at the moment of packing, you can envision this situation, put in the extra tote bag recommended to passionate shoppers in Chapter 3. Make sure it's well cushioned in whatever container you use. If you have purchased something unusual in size or shape, call the airline to confirm that you can bring it on board. Nowadays, since you're usually allowed only a single carry-on bag plus one personal item, you are going to have to think long and hard about what must travel in the cabin with you and what you're willing to consign to the cargo hold. In some instances, when an airport is on security alert, you may be allowed just one thing.

An alternative to shipping papers is to pack them flat in your luggage. But remember that they will add quite a bit of weight to the bag, and that you may not be able to lift it over your head into the overhead compartment of an airplane if you have to. Prepare to ask for help or store it under the seat in front of you.

▶ Souvenir Savvy

Consider the story of the dedicated shopper who buys a marble chessboard and chessmen, two porcelain plates, an alabaster candlestick, three prints, various odds and ends of jewelry, and a painted carnival mask on a trip to Italy. Marble being the weighty thing that it is, it's easy to imagine the havoc that could ensue en route inside the suitcase. If the lock should break with the weight of the marble, you can't count on a kind man at Alitalia to tie a stout rope around the bag and send it on. Anticipate your need for extra packing space on the return trip.

Don't learn the hard way about how to bring back souvenirs and gifts from afar without having an international packing incident.

DON'T BUY WHAT WON'T FIT The key to making sure all your purchases will go into your luggage is sometimes as simple as scale. Good things come in small packages: choose small items such as earrings or other jewelry. Prints are always good—they can be placed in an envelope for protection and packed flat, at least if you use a pullman. Scarves, ties, and sarongs make wonderful souvenirs and add almost no weight. T-shirts work, too.

ANTICIPATE SHOPPING FRENZIES If you know that you tend to fall helpless when your acquisitive impulses get going, simply pack an empty suitcase when you pack your clothing. Some shopaholics and other travel mavens actually fit the smaller suitcase inside the larger one on the outgoing trip.

If you want to make sure that something you purchase arrives home intact, you can try to carry it on board. Make sure it's well padded. If you have bought something unusual in size or shape, call the airline to confirm that you can bring it on board. Jumbo shopping bags containing large cardboard boxes usually won't work. In rare instances, when an airport is on security alert, you may be allowed just one thing rather than the more usual one carry-on plus one personal item combo. In any event, ship large items if possible. If you've done your buying in a country where shopkeepers neatly wrap every purchase, realize that the boxes may have to be unwrapped at security.

THE SHIPPING OPTION Do remember that sending your purchases home is always an option. If you insure the package and it is damaged, you will be reimbursed.

U.S. Customs permits travelers to send packages home duty-free: up to $200 worth of goods for personal use, with a limit of one parcel per addressee per day (and no alcohol or tobacco products or perfume worth more than $5). So if you see during your trip that you're getting close to the $400 limit, sort through your stuff and see what you can mail. Mark the package PERSONAL USE, and attach a list of its contents and their retail value. Do not label the package UNSOLICITED GIFT, or your duty-free exemption will drop to $100. Most reputable stores will handle the mailing for you. Your best choices are bulky or heavy items that will fit less readily in your luggage on the return trip.

ABOUT TRANSPORTING LIQUOR Have liquor packed by the merchant in a cardboard carrier—it's a lot easier to transport and show to customs. And always bring champagne aboard with you. It needs the pressurized air of the cabin.

▶ VAT Refunds and Customs

Frequent overseas travelers know that certain techniques can eliminate at least some of the hassles when leaving your destination and arriving back in the United States.

DON'T BUY WHAT YOU CAN'T KEEP There's a long list of items that cannot be brought into the United States. You can get a complete rundown from the U.S. Customs Web site. If you think you might acquire anything rare or unusual while you're away, it's a good idea to check it out in advance. Banned items include products made from wildlife or fish or from endangered species such as tortoiseshell or coral jewelry; ivory, unless it's antique and is properly documented as such; some types of ceramic tableware, which may contain high levels of lead; and some archaeological or ethnographic items such as masks or sculpture, from certain countries in Latin America and Africa. Cuban cigars are currently verboten.

KEEP RECEIPTS CLOSE AT HAND If you've been abroad, use one of the manila envelopes or resealable plastic bags from your portable office to hold receipts of purchases you've made. On the way home, keep the receipts where they're handy, with your travel documents. This will make things a lot easier if you're applying for an exemption from value-added taxes (VAT) in your country—always a good idea, since VATs of 15% or 20% can really add up on expensive items. Check your travel guide regarding procedures for the country you're visiting. In most countries, you need to get a special VAT-exempt invoice at the point of purchase, then present it to customs officials at your point of departure; your sales tax refund will be mailed to you later, or you may be given a voucher that will allow you to collect the rebate at an airport bank branch before you leave the country.

The envelope of receipts will also come in handy when you pass through U.S. Customs on your way home. Keep it with you on the plane so you can fill out your customs declaration card in flight. Try to pack purchases in one bag, if possible. Again, this saves time should you be asked to present them for inspection.

GET THE VAT REFUND YOU DESERVE The Value-Added Tax (also known as VAT) imposed on purchases by most European countries and some other nations is often a steep levy of up to 20%. What many American travelers don't know is that you can get it back when you leave the country under a refund program intended to benefit tourists.

It works like this: when making a purchase, find out whether the merchant gives refunds and ask for a VAT refund form. (Not all stores provide this service.) Then, get to the airport 30 minutes earlier to allow yourself time to get your refund. Have the store form stamped like any customs form by customs officials when you leave the country or when you leave the European Union if you're visiting several EU countries. Be ready to show customs officials what you've bought (pack purchases together in your carry-on luggage). After you're through passport control, take the form to a refund-service counter for an on-the-spot refund, or mail it back to the store or a refund service after you arrive home.

A refund service can save you some hassle, for a fee. Global Refund is a worldwide service with 130,000 affiliated stores and refund counters at major airports and border crossings. The service issues refunds in the form of cash, check, or credit-card adjustment, minus a processing fee. If you don't have time to wait at the refund counter, you can mail in the form instead. Is the money worth the hassle? Generally, it makes the most sense for big-ticket items. (In fact, most countries won't allow you to get a refund for small purchases.) But often the tax bite is big enough to repay your effort—in European nations, it ranges from 11.5% to 20%.

5

BAGGAGE PROBLEMS?

Were you left bagless at the carousel like a jilted bride at the altar? Did your brand-new Tumi emerge with a huge gash down the side? Worse still is when your luggage doesn't roll down the carousel—and you never see it again. Whatever the problem, make it a goal to start dealing with any problems you encounter on the spot, before you leave the airport.

▶ The Drill

No matter what the situation, it's sensible to keep a log of your interactions with the airline. Start a paper trail immediately. Don't leave the airport without filling out all required paperwork. Get copies of all forms. Get a receipt for your baggage tags when you hand them over. If you have a picture of your suitcases in your carry-on, you will be ahead of the game.

CATCH FLIES WITH HONEY If you have problems at any stage of the game, be calm, polite, and persistent. If you think you are getting nowhere, ask politely to speak with a supervisor. Ask again, if need be. Mentally review the points you'd like to make, and outline your ideas as clearly and quietly as you can when the supervisor arrives. Listen carefully and respond calmly.

DOCUMENT IT Make careful notes of any conversations you have then and later—who you talked to and when, as well as the highlights of your discussion and their contact information. Follow up with a letter—certified if it contains deadlined material. Include your daytime phone number on your letter; send a copy to the travel agent who booked your trip. If you have to spend money, keep receipts. If there are airline deadlines for filing forms or providing certain information, don't miss them or you risk damaging your case. Finally, ask what will happen when your luggage is found.

BUT IS IT LEGIBLE?

Make sure you can read the name of the person who signs on behalf of the airline; get his or her mailing address and direct phone number (you will encounter only frustration if you have only the reservations number), even if you're told your suitcase will be on the next plane.

▶ Damaged?

When you haul your bag off the carousel, give it a quick once-over to make sure there's no obvious damage. If there is, or if it's no longer locked, open it and look inside to make sure the contents are intact. If there are problems, contact the airline immediately—don't wait until you get home.

Even if it looks just as it did when you turned it over to the airline, survey the contents carefully as soon as you're settled and tell the airline if anything is missing. This is a case to follow up with a certified letter.

Airlines usually cover repairs to luggage they've mauled. You'll have to negotiate if the problem can't be fixed. For suitcases as for their contents, the airline will aim to cover only the depreciated value, not the replacement cost.

▶ Delayed?

When your luggage doesn't come off the carousel as it's supposed to, don't immediately assume that you'll never see it again. Airlines do succeed in tracking down about 98% of the bags they misplace and reunite most with their owners within 24 hours. Your immediate tasks are to replace necessary items you may need and to complete the required paperwork.

REUNION Depending on the circumstances, most airlines deliver lost-and-found bags without charge. If, for example, a last-minute check-in resulted in your bags going astray, the airline may be within its rights to charge you for delivery. Again, it all depends on the details. If you arrived at the airport at the recommended time and checked in late because of unusually long lines, you could argue persuasively that it was not your fault.

REIMBURSEMENT Until your luggage is returned to you, airlines do reimburse you for expenses you incur while your belongings are missing, although there are no legal requirements that they do so. Policies vary from company to company and situation to situation, from money to purchase a basic overnight kit containing personal items to partial reimbursement for clothing or other more substantial items. Some give you $25 for the first 24 hours your bag is missing; others reimburse you later for a percentage of your expenses, provided they are reasonable and backed by receipts. Some of this depends on whether you are away from home and how long it takes to track down your bags and return them to you. Some situations elicit more sympathy than others, and often the airport staff has wide discretion. Always make your case for the maximum you think you are owed.

If your carrier loses your skis or other sporting equipment you must have on your trip, the cost of renting replacements may be covered. But if you need new clothes, you may be able to collect only part of the cost—the thinking is that you can use the clothes again after your trip. If your luggage contained fresh foods that rotted because of the delayed delivery, the airline covers nothing.

KNOW YOUR RIGHTS Studying the airline's voluntary customer service guidelines or its conditions of carriage on its Web site will give you the full picture of what the airline will do for you in a variety of circumstances, in great detail. (Search for "customer service" or "carriage.") If you and the airline don't agree on what is reasonable, ask the agent you're dealing with to bring out a supervisor. Some airlines actually require that they be consulted before you make a purchase that you will later ask them to pay for. Be prepared to argue your case. You will either get a cash advance or a promise that you will be reimbursed later for any necessities you had to buy.

▶ Officially Lost?

If your bag lands in the "officially lost" column, you need to submit a formal claim. You will have to fill out a second, and much more detailed, form with estimates of the worth of all the items you packed, plus the value of the luggage itself. If you flew on more than one airline, you need to file the claim only with the carrier operating the final leg of your trip.

WHAT TO EXPECT Don't assume that the airline will pay the entire amount of the claim—expect to negotiate. Any sales receipts or other documentation you can muster to substantiate the value of the contents of your suitcase will be useful, especially if a large amount of money is involved; if you have saved all your receipts for purchases made before and during your trip that you put in your checked luggage, you'll be glad you did.

GET THE RIGHT SETTLEMENT The final offer will be based on the depreciated value of your suitcase and its contents, as with a damaged suitcase. Expect to wait between six weeks and three months to see a penny. The settlement may be in cash or a higher amount in the form of free travel on future flights. Before you jump at any free-travel deal, find out where you can use the ticket and ask about black-out periods, limits on when you can book, and other restrictions. The best offer is for anywhere on the airline's route system, including foreign destinations. The value of the tickets will ultimately depend on where you go, so don't undercut yourself by accepting travel vouchers in lieu of cash, then using them to travel a route where low-cost tickets abound.

NEED TO GO TO A HIGHER AUTHORITY? If the situation is not resolved, complain calmly and politely in writing, stating your expectations. If you don't think the response to your letter deals appropriately with your complaint, then send it to the Department of Transportation.

LUGGAGE & PACKING
RESOURCES

On-line catalogs and mail-order operations make it easier than ever to get organized and get going. Luggage manufacturers usually publish brochures containing detailed descriptions with photos or drawings of every suitcase they make and can provide names of retailers where you can examine the products firsthand. Catalogs, on-line and on paper, are invaluable as well.

Guidebooks

Fodor's Gold Guides

Fodor's flagship series of guidebooks covers destinations around the world. Each volume is loaded with tips and hints, including solid information about what to wear and what the weather will be like. Most have excellent information about water potability, diaper and film availability, electrical current and plug styles, and other essential bits.

Fodor's FYI Guides

Simple and easy to read, Fodor's FYI Guides are packed with tips, hints, checklists, and—plenty of packing information: *Plan Your Honeymoon*, *Travel with Your Baby*, *Plan and Enjoy Your Cruise*, and *Travel Fit and Healthy*.

Fodor's Languages for Travelers

If you decide to take phrase books, *Fodor's French for Travelers*, *Fodor's German for Travelers*, *Fodor's Italian for Travelers*, and *Fodor's Spanish for Travelers* will do the trick. For each title, there's a phrasebook/dictionary, along with a combination package that also includes either two audiocassettes or two CDs.

fodors.com

If you don't find what you need in this book, search the posts in the TravelTalk section of Fodor's Web site, or put up a question of your own. Very often you'll get a solid answer within the day from a fellow traveler who has just been there, done that. Click on Smart Travel Tips on the home page, and then on topic-specific buttons for helpful links.

Family Stuff

Crayola

crayola.com
1100 Church Lane
Easton, PA 18044-0431
610/253–6271
fax 610/250–5768

The venerable crayon maker has tuned into the travel market. Crayola Color Wonder products (there's a whole line of options) reduce road-trip mess stress because the colorless ink inside Color Wonder markers magically appears *only* on special Color Wonder paper. No more pink blobs on your new beige car seats.

http://stickygames.com

Makes and sells checkers, chess, and backgammon sets that use Velcro to keep pieces in place—perfect for trips.

General Packing Tips

Unclaimed Baggage Center

unclaimedbaggage.com
509 West Willow St.
Scottsboro, AL 35768
256/259–1525

The packing tips come from a unique perspective on the Web site of this Alabama store (which sells merchandise and clothing from baggage that has been officially declared unclaimed).

Government Resources

Aviation Consumer Protection Division

dot.gov/airconsumer
U.S. Department of Transportation
400 Seventh St., SW
Washington, DC 20590
202/366–2220

U.S. airlines' customer-service commitments are at dot.gov/airconsumer/customerservice.htm. The site also publishes statistics on bumping and oversells; a series of fact sheets called "Plane Talk" on topics ranging from frequent-flier plans to baggage to passengers with disabilities; and "Consumers Tell It to the Judge," about how to negotiate in small claims court. All of these are available on the Web at dot.gov/airconsumer/pubs.htm and dot.gov/airconsumer/telljudge.htm.

Federal Aviation Administration (FAA)

faa.gov
800 Independence Ave., SW
Washington, DC 20591
202/366–4000 or 800/255–1111
800/322–7873 Consumer Hotline

866/289–9673 Transportation Security Hotline
800/255–1111 Aviation Safety Hotline for time-critical events

Current information on airport procedures, airline regulations, forbidden carry-ons, and more.

U.S. Customs Service

customs.ustreas.gov
Box 7407
Washington, DC 20044

Links to useful publications, such as the fact-packed "Know Before You Go," a classic that's mandatory reading if you're headed overseas. The URL is customs.ustreas.gov/travel/travel.htm.

U.S. Department of State

travel.state.gov
202/647–5225

Publishes a number of useful information sheets, including consular information on many countries. Also good: "Your Trip Abroad," "A Safe Trip Abroad," and various sheets containing regional travel tips.

Laptop Needs

Belkin Components
belkin.com
Box 5649
Compton, CA 90224-5649
310/898-1100, 800/523-5546
fax 310/898-1111

On-line retailer with large
selection of computer cases.

Brenthaven
brenthaven.com
300 Harris Ave.
Bellingham, WA 98225
360/752-5537, 888/212-5301
fax 360/752-3362
consinfo@brenthaven.com

Serious laptop cases.

Meritline.com
meritline.com
16666 E. Johnson Dr.
City of Industry, CA 91745
626/369-8838, 888/668-6660
fax 626/369-8831
support@meritline.com

On-line retailer of numerous
manufacturers' laptop cases.

Pelican
laptop-cases-by-pelican.com
3370 Nacagdoches Rd., #1165
San Antonio, TX 78217-3371

800/666-6200
fax 210/590-9482
sales@pelican-case.com

On-line catalog of watertight
and airtight padded laptop cases.

Roadwired
roadwired.com
235 Middle Rd.
Henrietta, NY 14467
585/334-6960
fax 585/334-6962
customerservice@roadwired.com

Manufacturer and retailer of
cases for laptops and all other
kinds of electronic equipment.
Also sells ingenious high-tech
Velcro-closing equipment
wraps.

Targus
targus.com
1211 N. Miller St.
Anaheim, CA 92806
714/765-5555
fax 714/765-5599

Manufacturer and retailer of
equipment for mobile
computing, including laptop
cases and accessories, power
converter cords, and
connectivity devices.

Luggage Information

Travel Goods Association
travel-goods.org
5 Vaughn Dr., Ste. 105
Princeton, NJ 08540
609/720-1200
fax 609/720-0620

Can help you find a retailer
near you or get in touch

with manufacturers or luggage-
repair services and suppliers.
Provides general information
on innovative products, airline
carry-on regulations, leather
terminology, and preventing
luggage theft.

Passport Information

National Passport Center
travel.state.gov/
passport_services.html
603/334–0500,
888/362–8668

American Passport Service
americanpassport.com
603/431–8482, 800/841–6778

Express Visa Services
expressvisa.com
7 locations, including

18 E. 41st St., Ste. 1206
New York, NY 10017
212/679–5650

Passport Express
passportexpress.com
401/272–4612, 800/362–8196
179 Wayland Ave.
Providence, RI 02906

Travisa
travisa.com
800/222–2589, 800/421–5468

Technology Items and Info

iGo
igoproducts.com
9393 Gateway Dr.
Reno, NV 89511
775/850–2545, 800/422–9872
fax 775/850–9490, 800/232–
9229
igo@igoproducts.com

On-line mobile technology tools
and products for traveling with a
laptop, phone, and other devices.

http://kropla.com
Steve Kropla has created a Web
site full of information about
telephones and electricity
abroad—about international
dialing, mobile phones outside
the United States, electrical
current and plug styles, and more.

Laptop Travel
laptoptravel.com
Box 46106
Plymouth, MN 55446
763/404–9497, 888/527–8728
fax 763/404–9496, 800/409–
2449
mail@laptoptravel.com

Web site that sells products and
offers tips and tech support to
help you take your computer on
the road.

RoadNews.com
roadnews.com
Box 14524
Scottsdale, AZ 85267
480/225–8430
blethen@roadnews.com

Web resource with articles,
products, tips, and links to
other sites related to traveling
with technology.

teleadapt
teleadapt.com
1762 Technology Dr., Suite 223
San Jose, CA 95110
408/350–1440, 877/835–3232
fax 408/350–0160
info@teleadapt.com

On-line site offering
connectivity tips and products
for traveling with technology.

Travel Goods Manufacturers and National Retailers

Andiamo Luggage
andiamoinc.com
3011 S. Crobdy Way
Santa Ana, CA 92704-6304
714/751–8711, 800/759–9738
fax 714/751–4703

Luggage manufacturer. Product and on-line catalog available.

Atlantic Luggage Company
atlanticluggage.com
10th St. and Factory Ave.
Ellwood City, PA 16117-0672
724/752–0012, 888/285–2684
fax 724/752–3444
info@atlanticluggage.com

Luggage manufacturer with on-line catalog.

Backpack Traveler
europebytrain.com
Box 3538
Dana Point, CA 92629
949/661–9577, 800/688–9577
fax 949/488–9577
inquire@europebytrain.com

Catalog retailer with an on-line catalog. Sells packs and other luggage, plus travel gadgets.

Boyt
boyt.com
15 Sarah Ave.
Iowa Falls, IA 50126-0279
641/648–6601, 888/289–2698
fax 641/648–2385

Luggage manufacturer. Product and on-line catalog available.

Briggs & Riley
briggs-riley.com
Box 3169
Half Moon Bay, CA 94019
650/728–2000, 888/462–2247
fax 650/728–2002
contactus@briggs-riley.com

Manufacturer of stylish soft-side luggage. Product catalog available on request and on-line.

Brookstone
brookstone.com
800/846–3000

This e-tailer/retailer includes luggage and travel gadgets in its intriguing stock.

Bugatti, Inc.
bugatti.com
100 Condor St.
Boston, MA 02128
617/567–7600, 800/284–2887
fax 617/567–5541
leather@bugatti.com

Manufacturer of leather casual bags and accessories with on-line catalog sales.

800-LUGGAGE
1800luggage.com
656 S. Pickett St.
Alexandria, VA 22304
703/751–1109, 800/584–4243
fax 703/751–1346
customer-service@
1800luggage.com

Washington, D.C.–area luggage discount retailer with on-line catalog (order by phone).

Cascade Designs

cascadedesigns.com
4000 First Ave. S.
Seattle, WA 98134
800/531–9531
fax 800/583–7583

Manufactures the Packtowl® as well as an award-winning water purification system, state-of-the-art camping mattresses, and other innovative items.

The Container Store

thecontainerstore.com
2000 Valwood Parkway
Dallas, TX 75234
888/266–8246

This nationwide chain with an on-line presence is a ready source of tiny bottles and jars that are perfect for your toilet kit. You'll also find many travel gadgets, though this is by no means the ultimate resource for that.

CrewGear

crewgear.com
10855 U.S. 19N
Clearwater, FL 33764
800/848–2739
fax 800/329–5387

Sells luggage and travel products to airline crews and general public. Product catalog available on request and on-line (phone ordering only).

Croakies

croakies.com
1240 Huff Lane
Box 2913
Jackson Hole WY 83001
800/443–8620

Original manufacturers of neoprene eyewear retainers.

Delsey Luggage

delsey.com
6735 Business Pkwy. Ste. A
Elkridge, MD 21075
410/796–5655, 800/558–3344
fax 410/796–4192

Manufacturer of innovative, hard- and soft-side luggage. Catalog available.

Eddie Bauer

eddiebauer.com
Box 97000
Redmond, WA 98073-9700
425/641–2564, 800/426–8020,
customer service 800/625–7935
fax 425/806–7851, 800/414–6110
custsat@ebauer.com

Retailer with on-line catalog sales, mail-order catalog, and stores nationwide.

Goods of the World

travelbags.com
3101 E. Eisenhower Pkwy.
Ann Arbor, MI 48108
734/677–0700, 800/950–2247
fax 734/941–8543

Manufacturer of leather bags for travel and sports. Catalog available on request.

Hartmann Luggage Company

hartmann.com
1301 Hartmann Dr.
Lebanon, TN 37087
615/444–5000, 800/331–0613
fax 888/443–5409

Luggage manufacturer. Mail order and on-line catalog available.

Innovation Luggage

20 Enterprise Ave. S
Secaucus, NJ 07094
800/722–1800

Luggage-specialist retailer carrying major brands. List of stores available by phone; no catalog.

Lands' End Direct Merchants

landsend.com
1 Lands' End La.
Dodgeville, WI 53595
608/935–6170, 800/356–4444
fax 800/332–0103
mailbox@landsend.com

Catalog and on-line retailer with a selection of luggage, backpacks, and attachés, along with casual clothing.

L.L. Bean

llbean.com
Freeport, ME 04033
207/552–3028, 800/221–4221
fax 207/552–3080
llbean@llbean.com

Venerable retailer with catalog, on-line sales, and stores. Sells outdoor gear and clothing, including luggage, packs, and accessories.

Lodis

lodis.com
2261 S. Carmelina Ave.
Los Angeles, CA 90064-1001
310/207–6841, 800/421–8674

Laptop cases, hands-free bags, small leather accessories, and travel items.

Magellan's

magellans.com
110 W. Sola St.
Santa Barbara, CA 93101-3007
805/568–5400, 800/962–4943
fax 805/568–5406, 800/962–4940
customerservice@magellans.com

Catalog and on-line retailer with a huge selection of travel supplies, everything from adapters and converters to water filters, language translators, packing aids, and travel-friendly clothing.

McKlein USA

mckleinusa.com
964 Northpoint Blvd.
Waukegan, IL 60085
847/785–1715, 877/625–5346
fax 847/785–1714

Manufactures luggage for traveling professionals.

Orvis Travel

orvis.com
1711 Blue Hills Dr.
Box 12000
Roanoke, VA 24012
800/541–3541, customer service 800/635–7635
fax 540/343–7053

Retailer with catalog and stores nationwide. Sells luggage, clothing, and accessories.

Samsonite
samsonite.com
11200 E. 45th Ave.
Denver, CO 80239
303/373–2000, 800/262–8282
fax 303/373–6300

Venerable luggage manufacturer with many innovative products. Product listing on request.

Sharper Image
sharperimage.com
Box 7031
San Francisco, CA 94120-9703
800/344–5555, 650/344–4444
fax 415/445–1584

The ultimate source of gadgetry.

Skymall
skymall.com
Box 52824
Phoenix, AZ 85072
602/254–9777, 800/424–6255
fax 602/528–3240, 800/986–6255

On-line and product catalog retailer; catalog is available in airplane seat backs or on special request by phone. Travel gear.

Tilley Endurables
tilley.com
900 Don Mills Rd.
Toronto, ON M3C 1V6
Canada
416/441–6141, 800/363–8737
tilley@tilley.com

High-performance travel clothing is the specialty of this company built around a sailing hat; most Tilley gear dries overnight even under humid conditions.

Title 9 Sports
title9sports.com
6201 Doyle St.
Emeryville, CA 94608
800/342–4448

Casual performance wear for women—lots of Supplex and Cool Max.

Travel 2000
travel2000.com
3120 Spanish Oak Dr.
Lansing, MI 48911
517/882–2988, 800/903–8728
fax 517/882–1094

Catalog retailer with luggage and travel gear.

Travelers Club
travelersclub.com
13003 S. Figueroa St.
Los Angeles, CA 90061
310/323–5660, 800/368–2582
fax 310/323–5825
info@travelersclub.com

Luggage manufacturer and wholesaler with on-line catalog.

Travelpro
travelpro.com
700 Banyan Tr.
Boca Raton, FL 33431
561/998–2824, 800/741–7471
fax 561/998–8487

Luggage manufacturer with catalog. Web page lists international resources.

TravelSmith
travelsmith.com
60 Leveroni Ct.
Nevato, CA 94949
415/382–1855, 800/950–1600
fax 800/950–1656
service@travelsmith.com

Catalog retailer specializing in
luggage and travel accessories.
On-line product catalog (order
by phone).

Tumi
tumi.com
800/332–8864

One of the first companies to
make black-on-black suitcases,
Tumi manufactures well-
designed luggage for affluent
travelers. Founded in 1975 by a
former Peace Corps volunteer
who imported leather bags from
Colombia, it was named after a
Peruvian god.

Walkabout Travel Gear
walkabouttravelgear.com
Box 1115
Moab, UT 84532
435/259–4974, 800/852–7085
fax 530/658–8772
sales@walkabouttravelgear
.com

Catalog and on-line retailer of
luggage and travel gadgets and
gear.

Zero Halliburton
zerohalliburton.com
500 W. 200 N
N. Salt Lake, UT 84054
801/298–5900, 888/909–9376
fax 801/936–2296
info@zerohalliburton.com

Manufacturer of classic
aluminum suitcases and
briefcases. Can provide a
catalog of products and names
of retailers near you.

Travel Insurance

Access America
accessamerica.com
800/284–8300

The Berkely Group
berkely.com
100 Garden City Plaza
Box 9366
Garden City, NY 11530
800/645–2424

Sells through tour operators
and travel agents.

CSA Travel Protection
Box 939057
San Diego, CA 92193-9057
800/873–9855

Travel Guard International
travel-guard.com
800/826–4919

Travel Insured
travelinsured.com
800/243–3174

Travelers Insurance Company is
the underwriter.

Travelex
travelex-insurance.com
800/797–4515

The former Mutual of Omaha;
acquired Thomas Cook Global
& Financial Services in 2001.

Travel Packs and Outdoor Gear

Campmor
campmor.com
201/445–5000, 800/226–7667
fax 201/689–9678

Catalog retailer with one store
(Route 17 North, Paramus,
New Jersey) and on-line catalog
sales. Luggage and gear for
outdoor activities and more.

Due North Outdoor Supplies
duenorth.net/outdoor
11345 Hwy. 17 W
Box 6264
Sturgeon Falls, Ont. P2B 3K7
Canada
705/753–2387
fax 705/753–6113
sales@duenorth.com

Canada-based on-line catalog
retailer of packs and other
camping gear.

Eagle Creek Travel Gear
eaglecreek.com
3055 Enterprise Ct.
Vista, CA 92083
760/599–6500, 800/874–9925
fax 800/874–1038

Travel luggage and gear
manufacturer. Product catalog
and list of retailers available on
request or on-line.

Eastern Mountain Sports
emsonline.com
1 Vose Farm Rd.
Peterborough, NH 03458-2122
888/463–6367
fax 603/924–4320
customerservice@emsonline.com

Outdoor gear retailer with on-
line catalog (order by phone)
and stores nationwide.

High Sierra Sport Company
highsierrasport.com
880 Corporate Woods Park
Vernon Hills, IL 60061
800/323–9590

JanSport
jansport.com
Box 1817
Appleton, WI 54912
920/734–5708, 800/552–6776
fax 920/831–2367

Manufacturer of travel packs
and travel and outdoor
accessories. Product information
and dealer names on-line and
on request.

Patagonia
patagonia.com
Box 32050
Reno, NV 89523-2050
800/638–6464, 800/336–9090
catalog requests
fax 800/543–5522

Manufacturer of outdoor gear,
including luggage, backpacks,
and accessories, with retail
stores and complete on-line
and mail-order catalogs.

REI
rei.com
1700 45th St. E
Sumner, WA 98352-0001
253/891–2500, 800/426–4840
fax 253/891–2523
service@rei.com

Manufacturer of outdoor gear
and clothing with retail stores,
catalog, and on-line sales.

VAT Refunds

Global Refund
globalrefund.com
99 Main St., Ste. 307
Nyack, NY 10960
800/566–9828, 845/348–7673
fax 845/348–1549

Weather

CNN Weather
cgi-cnn.com/weather

**National Oceanic
and Atmospheric
Administration**
noaa.com
202/482–6090

National Weather Service
nationalweatherservice.com

USA Today Weather
usatoday.com/weather/
wfront.htm

Weather Channel
weather.com

Index

A

Accessories
garment bag accessories, 131
luggage accessories, 90
men, 40
resources for, 168, 170, 171, 172
wardrobe options, 40, 43–44, 48
women, 48
Adapters, 65, 85, 88–89, 90–91, 170
Adventure trips, 50–57
cold weather, 54–56
day packs, 51
hot weather, 51–53
luggage, 50–51
mountain trips, 56–57
Africa, 50, 155
Air travel. ☞ *Also* Carry-on luggage; Checking luggage
babies and toddlers, 70, 71, 73
baggage rules, 80–83
closet availability, 83
comfort while flying, 140–141
computers and security, 19, 136–137
delayed flights, 140
entertainment while flying, 88–90
flight confirmations, 139
food, 83, 141–142
planning, 80–86
security, 19, 99, 101, 102, 106, 136–137
travel outfit for, 45
Airport codes, 145
Alaska, 64
Alcohol, shipping, 154, 155
Aluminum suitcases, 10, 172
Antigua, 88
Antiques, 61, 145

Archaeological items, 155
Argentina, 88
Asia, 114
ATMs, 87
Australia, 89
Aviation Consumer Protection Division, 165

B

Baby wipes, 100
Backpacks. ☞ *See* Travel packs
Baggage. ☞ *Also* Checking luggage
rules for, 80–83
unclaimed, 165
Bahamas, 89
Banned items, 155
Bathing suits, 75, 140
Bermuda, 89
Bicycles/Bicycling, 60, 147
Bowling balls, 147
Burlington, Vermont, 145
Business customs, 58
Business documents, 139
Business trips, 57–60
fitness, 59
luggage, 59–60
packing, 58
packing paper for return trip, 152–153
relaxation, 58–59
shoes, 59
women's business wear, 48

C

Cable ties, 146–147
Cameras, 53, 54, 55, 57, 62, 76, 93, 139
Camping gear, 169, 173

Canada, 89, 147
Car seats, 70
Car trips, 62, 72
Caribbean, 67, 75, 88, 89, 114, 140
Carry-on luggage
    buying, 20–23
    checking, 137–140
    etiquette, 142
    garment bags as, 13–14
    heavy articles, 136
    lists for, 138, 139
    packing, 22, 136–142
    problems with, 82–83, 140
    at security checkpoints, 136–137
    size, 21–22
    sturdiness, 22–23
    tips for, 84
    toiletries kit, 103
    wardrobe considerations, 38–39
Cash, 87, 113–114, 145
Casual vacations, 60–62
    antiquing, 61
    eating out, 61
    golf and tennis, 60
    horseback riding, 61
    jackets for, 61
    luggage, 62
    packing, 62
    picnics, 61
    walking and bicycling, 60
Ceramics, 155
Checking luggage, 143–148
    carry-ons, 137–140
    closing luggage, 148
    identifying luggage, 145–146
    insurance, 143, 145
    items not to check, 138–140
    locking luggage, 146–147
    luggage tags, 147
    responsibilities of travelers, 147
    security checkpoints, 136–137

    special items, 83, 147
    tips for, 144, 146
    value of luggage, 143, 145
    weight and size limits, 83, 144, 147
Checklists, 116
    carry-on contents, 138, 139
    carry-on tips, 84
    checked-luggage tips, 146
    cold weather packing, 56
    day pack ideas, 51
    first-aid kit, 107
    hot weather packing, 53
    kid stuff, 68–69
    laptop cases, 19
    laundry kit, 104
    luggage features, 24
    men's wardrobe, 40–41
    mountain trips, 57
    night-before to-do list, 115
    personal documents kit, 109
    portable office, 110–111
    pretrip to-do list, 113
    sewing kit, 105
    shopper's survival kit, 112
    stress-free packing, 79
    toiletries kit, 99
    toy totes, 72
    travel aids, 94
    wardrobe planning, 32
    what to wear during flights, 45
    women's wardrobe, 48–49
Children. ☞ Also Family vacations
    air travel, 70, 71, 73
    car seats, 70–72
    diapers, 66–67
    duffels for, 10
    packing for, 68–69
    toy totes, 70
Chile, 88
Cigars, 155

City vacations, 62–63
camera, 62
evening wear, 63
layering, 63
local customs, 63
luggage, 63
safety, 63
shoes and walking, 62
umbrella, 63
Clothing retailers, 170, 171, 173
Clothing sizes, 46
Clothing-store method, 132, 134
Cold weather
adventure travel, 54–56
packing list for, 56
theme park vacations, 77
Computer cases, 17–20, 136–137, 166, 170
Computers
airport security and, 19, 136–137
travel products for, 167
Conditions of carriage, 83
Consular information, 165
Contact lenses, 100
Converters, 65, 85, 88–89, 90–91, 170
Coral, 155
Crayola, 71, 164
Cribs, 147
Croakies, 50, 169
Cruises, 64–65
electricals, 65
evening wear, 64–65
luggage, 65
safety, 65
shore excursions, 64
swimming and sports, 64
Customs
business customs, 58
clothing customs, 85
local customs, 34–35, 52, 63

Customs Service, U.S., 147, 154–155, 156, 165

D

Day packs, 17, 51
Dehydration, 140–141
Dental floss, 97, 106, 131
Denver, Colorado, 145
Desert travel, 50, 51–52, 53
Diapers, 66–67
Diving, 53
Double stack method, 122–125
Dresses, 7, 42, 48
Dressmaker's dummy, 124, 129–130
Dry-cleaner bags, 120, 124, 126–127, 132, 151
Dry-cleaner method, 132–133, 134
Duct tape, 148
Duffels
for adventures trips, 51
buying, 10–12
as carry-ons, 20–21
for casual vacations, 62
colors, 12
converting to packs, 11–12
inside features, 11–12
packing, 125–126
size, 11
weight distribution, 125–126
zone system, 126
Duty-free shipping exemption, 154–155
DVD player, 73

E

Electricals, 65, 85, 88–89, 90–91, 170
Equipment wraps, 166
Ethnographic items, 155
Europe, 34, 38, 62, 63, 67, 101, 114, 156–157

European Union, 156
Evening wear
city vacations, 63
cruises, 64–65
men, 41
resort vacations, 75
women, 49
Excess valuation insurance, 143,
145
Exercise, 59, 64
Eyewear, 50, 98, 100, 139, 169

F

Fairchild, Patricia, 95
Family vacations, 66–74
car seats, 70
checklist for, 68–69
clothes and useful items, 76
comfort objects, 74
diapers, 66–67
entertainment, 73
food and drink, 70
luggage, 74
one-parent trips abroad, 74
teenagers, 66
toy totes, 70–72
Federal Aviation Administration
(FAA), 167
Film, 55, 93
Film canisters, 127
First-aid kit, 50, 106–107
Fishing poles, 147
Fitness, 59, 64
Flashlight, 51
Florida, 75, 76–77, 145
Fodor's, 164
Folding methods, 132–136
clothing-store method, 132,134
dry-cleaner method, 132–133, 134
long-sleeve sweaters, 133
slacks, 133
stack-and-fold method, 133, 134–135
sun hat, 136

Food, 70, 83, 141–142, 161
Foreign currency, 113–114
Fragile items, 147
France, 67, 89

G

Gadgets, 168, 169, 171, 172
Games, 164
Garment bags, 113
accessories for, 131
avoiding wrinkles, 129, 131
for business trips, 59–60
buying, 12–14
as carry-on, 13–14, 21–22
dressmaker's dummy, 129, 130
hardware, 29–30
opening style of, 14
packing, 126–131
on return trip, 151
shoes in, 131
size of, 12
variations, 14
what not to pack, 131
Germany, 89
Gifts, 85, 137, 139–140
Global Refund, 156–157, 174
Golf, 60, 64, 75, 147
Government resources, 165
Great Britain, 47, 58, 89, 145
Guadeloupe, 88
Guam, 89
Guidebooks, 34, 67, 84–85, 86,
164

H

Handbags, 60, 92
Handles, 27–28, 144
Hands-free bags, 170
Hartford, Connecticut, 145
Hats, 54, 136, 171
Hawaii, 75
Health matters, 87
Hiking, 56–57

Home preparations, 95
Homesickness/hominess, 112
Honduras, 88
Hong Kong, 89
Horseback riding, 61, 75
Hostess gifts, 85
Hot weather
adventure travel, 51–53
local customs, 35
packing list for, 53
theme park vacations, 76–77

I

Immersion heater, 91
Immigration requirements, 74
Insect repellent, 101–102
Insurance, 86, 143, 145, 172
Interlock method, 120–122
Ireland, 47
Ironing, 85, 115–116. ☞ Also
Wrinkles
Italy, 34, 63
Ivory, 155

J

Jackets, 42
for casual vacations, 61
folding, 120
men, 40
women, 48
Jamaica, 89, 140
Japan, 89
Jeans, 8, 43, 116, 120
Jewelry, 43–44, 63, 127, 138, 145
Jungle travel, 52

K

Kalamazoo/Battle Creek airport,
145
Knives, 101, 106, 142
Korea, 89
Kropla, Steve, 167

L

Language translators, 170
Laptops
in airports, 19
cases for, 17–20, 136–137, 166,
170
portable office and, 110
resources for, 166, 167
Las Vegas, Nevada, 145
Latin America, 155
Laundry, 85, 87, 91–92
return trip and, 150–151
wardrobe planning and, 39
Laundry kit, 73, 103–104
Layering, 50, 55, 56, 63
Leather items, 168, 169, 170
Leggings, 42
Lingerie, 41, 49
Liquor, transporting, 155
Local customs, 34–35, 52, 63
Locks, 26–27, 90, 146
Logo items, 44
London, England, 46, 47, 58, 145
Los Angeles, California, 145
Lost luggage, 95–97, 161–162
Luggage. ☞ Also Carry-on
luggage; Checking luggage
accessories for, 90
adventure travel, 50–51
alarm for, 90
business trips, 59–60
casual vacations, 62
city vacations, 63
cruises, 65
family vacations, 74
identification, 95–97, 144, 145–
146, 147
information about, 166
lost luggage, 95–97, 161–162
manufacturers and retailers, 168–
172
repair, 166
resort vacations, 76

soft-side, 8–9, 144
Luggage, buying, 1–30
  carry-on luggage, 20–23
  duffels, 10–12
  garment bags, 12–14
  laptop luggage, 17–20
  needs for luggage, 3–4
  price shopping, 8
  pullmans, 6–10
  quality, 23–30
  travel packs, 14–17
  trying out luggage, 5–6
  wheels, 5–6, 29
Luggage problems, 158–162
  avoiding, 159
  customer rights, 161
  damaged luggage, 162
  delayed luggage, 160–161
  documentation, 159
  lost luggage, 95–97, 161–162
  reimbursement, 160–161
  settlement, 162
Luggage quality, 23–30
  closings, 26
  construction, 24–25
  fabric, 25–26
  features, 24, 30
  frame, 24
  handles, 27–28
  hardware, 29–30
  locks, 26–27
  straps and webbing, 28–29, 90, 144
  waterproof/water-resistant, 26
  wheels, 29
Luggage tags, 90, 146, 147

M

Manhattan, 46
Manuscripts, 148
Maps, 86
Markers, 71, 164
Medications, 87, 137, 138

Mesh bags, 126
Mexico, 89, 75
Middle East, 34
Milan, Italy, 63
Millay, Edna St. Vincent, 37
Money matters, 87, 113–114, 145
Mountain trips, 56–57
Musical instruments, 83, 145, 147

N

Nail clippers, 137
Nashville, Tennessee, 145
Negotiable securities, 145
New Orleans, Louisiana, 145
New York City, 47
New York state, 46
New Zealand, 89
Noise, 90

O

Oman, 145
One-parent trips abroad, 74
Orlando, Florida, 76–77, 145
Outdoor gear and clothing, 169, 173
Outerwear, 41, 49

P

Packing, 117–142
  backwards packing, 151
  business trips, 58, 152–153
  carry-ons, 22, 136–142
  casual vacations, 62
  checklists for, 53, 56, 79, 116, 150
  countdown to, 113–116
  double stacks, 122–125
  duffels, 125–126
  filling the suitcase, 117–125
  folding methods, 132–135
  garment bags, 126–131
  interlock method, 120–122
  last in, first out, 118

the night before, 115–116
overpacking, 36–39
paper, for return trip, 152–153
pretrip to-do list, 113
return trips, 149–157
rolling method, 118–120
with shoes, 122
stress-free packing, 79
test run, 114
tight packing, 120
tips for, 165
tissue paper vs. plastic, 124
travel packs, 125–126
for two, 96
Packing aids, 170
Packing envelopes, 90, 126
Packs. ☞ *See* Day packs; Travel packs
Packtowel, 91, 169
Pants, 40, 42, 48, 120, 133
Paper, packing, 152–153
Paper clips, 146
Paperwork, 85–86
Paraguay, 88
Passports, 85–86, 108, 167
Perfume, shipping, 154
Personal documents kit, 107–109, 114, 139
Phoenix, Arizona, 46
Photo ID, 108
Photos/photography, 10, 54, 55, 57, 62, 76, 93, 139
Picnics, 61, 91
Pittsburgh, Pennsylvania, 145
Planning
air travel, 80–84
calling hotels, 85
electrical needs, 85
home preparations, 95
identifying your things, 95–97
insurance, 86
paperwork, 85–86

researching your needs, 84–86
shots, 86
studying the destination, 84–85
wardrobe, 33–47
water potability, 85
Plastic bags, 73, 91–92, 102, 114, 120, 124, 126, 132, 151
Plastic bottles and jars, 98, 169
Plastic vs. tissue paper, 124
Portable office, 109–111
Puerto Rico, 89
Pullmans
for business trips, 59–60
buying, 6–10
converting to a pack, 10
hard-side, 9–10
packing, 125
soft-side, 8–9
Pump dispensers, 98
Purses, 60, 92

Q

Quick-dry clothing, 50, 52, 54, 56, 77

R

Rafting, 50, 57
Rain, 42, 47, 52
Razors, 137
Receipts, 139, 155–156, 159, 161, 162
Resort vacations, 75–76
evening wear, 75
handy bring-alongs, 76
local customs, 34–35
luggage, 76
safety, 76
sports gear, 75
swimsuit protocols, 75
Resources, 163–174
family items, 164
government resources, 165

guidebooks, *164*
laptop needs, *165*
luggage information, *166*
packing tips, *165*
passports, *167*
technology items and information, *167*
travel goods manufacturers and
retailers, *168–172*
travel insurance, *172*
travel packs and outdoor gear, *173*
VAT refunds, *174*
weather, *174*
Restaurants, *61*
Return trips, *149–157*
dirty laundry, *150–151*
packing list for, *150*
paper, *152–153*
souvenirs, *153–155*
VAT refunds and customs, *155–157*
Rolling method, *118–120*
Rome, Italy, *34*

S

Safety, *92*
city vacations, *63*
cruises, *65*
resort vacations, *76*
Safety pins, *146*
Safety razors, *137*
St. Kitts/Nevis, *88*
St. Lucia, *88*
St. Vincent, *88*
San Francisco, California, *63*
Sanitary pads, *101*
Scarves, *42*
Scissors, *106*
Seasickness, *65, 87*
Security checkpoints, *19, 99, 101,
102, 106, 136–137*
Sentimental items, *138*
Sequined outfits, *127*
Sewing kit, *105–106*

Shaving, *100, 137*
Shipping, *154–155*
Shirts, *35, 40, 48, 118, 132–133*
Shoes, *39, 44*
adventure trips, *52, 54*
business trips, *59*
city vacations, *62*
cruises, *64*
in garment bags, *131*
men, *40*
packing with, *122*
rainproofing, *47*
theme park vacations, *77*
women, *48–49*
Shopper's survival kit, *111–112*
Shopping, *86–95*
comfort items, *92*
at destination, *93*
drugstore items, *87*
electricals, *88–89, 90–91*
entertainment items, *88–90*
guidebooks and maps, *86*
health items, *87*
for items left behind, *37, 84–85*
laundry items, *91–92*
luggage accessories, *90*
money matters, *87*
picnics and potables, *91*
for recording memories, *92–93*
safety items, *92*
souvenirs, *153–155*
staying in touch, *90*
travel aids, *94*
Shore excursions, *64*
Shorts, *52*
Shots, *86, 87*
Silk sleep sack, *92*
Singapore, *58*
Sizes
clothing, *46*
diapers, *67*
Skateboards, *147*

Skiing, *54, 55, 147, 161*
Skirts, *48, 120*
Slacks, *40, 42, 48, 120, 133*
Sleep sack, *92*
Sleepwear, *41, 49*
Snorkeling, *53*
Snowboarding, *55, 147*
Socks
adventures trips, 52
business trips, 59
city vacations, 62
men, 40
women, 49
Soft-side luggage, *8–9, 144*
Souvenirs, *153–155*
Sports gear, *64, 75, 147, 161*
camping and outdoor gear, 169, 173
men, 41
women, 49
Stack-and-fold method, *133, 134–135*
Stains, *103–104*
State Department, *165*
Stiller, Ben, *82–83*
Straps, *28–29, 90, 144*
Strollers, *83*
Suits, *7, 12–14, 40*
Summer. ☞ *See* Hot weather
Sun hats, *136*
Sunscreen, *76, 101, 103*
Sweaters
folding, 133
men, 40
women, 48
Swimsuits/swimming, *64, 75, 140*
Swiss Army knife, *101, 106*
Syringes, *137*

T

T-shirts, *8, 118, 119*
Tampons, *101*
Tank tops, *52*

Technology-related resources, *167*
Teenagers, *66*
Telephones, *167*
Tennis, *60, 75*
Theme park vacations, *76–77*
Tiaras, *127*
Ties, *127, 129*
Tipping, *113–114*
Tissue paper, *124*
Tissues, *92, 100*
Tobacco, shipping, *154*
Toiletries, *8, 131*
for children, 74
storing, 102
Toiletries kit, *97–103, 114, 169*
Toronto, Canada, *147*
Tortoiseshell, *155*
Tote bags, *70–72, 111, 153*
Tour vouchers, *139*
Towels, *91, 169*
Toy totes, *70–72*
Travel aids, *94, 131*
Travel documents, *139*
Travel goods, resources for, *168–172*
Travel journal, *92*
Travel kits, *97–112, 114*
first-aid kit, 106–107
laundry kit, 103–104
personal documents kit, 107–109
portable office, 109–111
sewing kit, 105–106
shopper's survival kit, 111–112
toiletries kit, 97–103
Travel packs, *21*
adventure trips, 50–51
buying, 14–17
distribute the weight, 125–126
features, 17
outside pockets, 126
packing, 125–126
resources for, 173
size, 16

structure, 16
zone system, 126
Travel-size products, 98
Tropics, 34, 50
Trousers, 40, 42, 48, 120, 133
Tweezers, 137
Twist-ties, 97, 131, 146–147

U

Umbrellas, 63, 137
Unclaimed baggage, 165
Underwear, 39, 41, 49
Uruguay, 88

V

Valuables, 138–139, 147
VAT refunds, 155–157, 174
VCRs, 73
Venice, Italy, 34
Virgin Islands, U.S., 89
Visas, 85–86
Voltage, 89–89

W

Walkie-talkies, 55, 90
Walking, 59, 60, 62
Walking canes, 137
Walt Disney World, 76–77
Wardrobe, 31–77
   accessories, 40, 43–44, 48
   adventure trips, 50–57
   business trips, 57–60
   casual vacations, 60–62
   checklists for, 32, 40–41, 48–49
   city vacations, 62–63
   color scheme, 42
   comfort factor, 35
   cruises, 64–65
   dressing for flights, 45

editing the clothing list, 44
   family vacations, 66–74
   how much to pack, 39
   laundry considerations, 39
   lightweight and wrinkleproof, 43
   local customs, 34–35
   logo items, 44
   men, 40–41
   multiclimate trip, 46–47
   overpacking, 36–37
   planning, 33–47
   for rain, 47
   resort vacations, 75–76
   theme park vacations, 76–77
   travel style, 35–36
   versatility of, 39, 42
   weather considerations, 45–47
   women, 48–49
Warsaw Convention, 143
Water, for hydration, 140–141
Water potability, 85, 91, 169, 173
Water sports, 75
Waterproofing, 26, 54
Weather
   cold weather, 54–56, 77
   hot weather, 35, 51–53, 76–77
   multiclimate trips, 46–47
   resources, 174
   wardrobe considerations, 45–47
Wheels, 5–6, 29, 59–60
Winter. ☞ See Cold weather
Workouts, 59, 64
Wrinkles, 8, 13, 43, 129–131
   folding methods, 132–136
   laundry kit, 103–104

Z

Zipper pulls, 27, 146
Zone system, 126